Jewish
Vegetarian
Cooking

Jewish Vegetarian Cooking

Rose Friedman

The official cookbook of the
International Jewish Vegetarian Society

Thorsons
An Imprint of HarperCollins*Publishers*

Thorsons
An Imprint of HarperCollins*Publishers*
77–85 Fulham Palace Road,
Hammersmith, London W6 8JB

First published by Thorsons 1984
7 9 10 8 6

A catalogue record for this book
is available from the British Library

ISBN 0 7225 2471 4

Typeset by Harper Phototypesetters Limited,
Northampton, England
Printed and bound in Great Britain by
Caledonian International Book Manufacturing Ltd,
Glasgow, G64

Contents

I should like to express my thanks and appreciation to my family, friends and everybody who has helped in the preparation of this book.

Rose Friedman

Foreword

Tradition in food is nurtured deep in the human psyche; through home influence and childhood days it casts its spell of happiness and security.

It is in the natural order of things, therefore, that a change in food habits is not easily brought about; the fact that the inherited pattern was not necessarily a good one is usually of little relevance. Most people look back to their childhood with longing, and the food their mothers prepared is usually something that remains near and dear to their hearts. Jewish philosophy has taken this factor fully into account and it has been incorporated into the very fabric of the Jewish faith. Partaking of food is a sacred right and the table becomes an altar dedicated to a service of thanksgiving.

The age-old tradition of liberal hospitality commences with Abraham and continues in every Jewish home. During the dispersion to many lands, tradition hallowed the various aspects of Jewish food and the best from each place of sojourn altered the pattern, but love, warmth and hospitality remained the essential ingredients.

The invitation by the publishers for the JVS to produce a traditional cookery book within the context of vegetarianism was therefore welcomed by the Society as satisfying readers' inherent love of their traditional background. Our publishers have thereby added one more star to their record of publications designed for thinking people who look upon health as a blessing and a return as far as possible to the appreciation of natural things.

The vegetarian alternatives will enable readers to enjoy the delights of their traditional dishes, knowing that they will be conducive to the good health of their families while carrying out the strictest requirements of Kashruth.

Their table will be adorned with the peaceful and goodly products of the land, thus hastening the days when 'they shall no longer hurt nor destroy'.

B'tayavon!

Philip L Pick
Hon. Life President,
The International Jewish Vegetarian Society

'I went down into the garden of nuts to see the fruits of the valley, and to see whether the vine had blossomed, whether the pomegranates were in flower.'

Song of Songs

About the International Jewish Vegetarian Society

The International Jewish Vegetarian and Ecological Society is represented worldwide and welcomes new members of all persuasions. The quarterly magazine, sent free to members, features articles on nutrition, health, travel, gardening, recipes, ethical and religious aspects of vegetarianism, with news from and about its many readers, as well as giving information about international developments and conferences.

Further information regarding membership of the Society, can be obtained from, and enquiries about matters related to this book can be directed to:

The International Jewish Vegetarian Society Headquarters
Bet Teva
853/855 Finchley Road
London NW11 8LX

or to:

The Jerusalem Centre
8 Balfour Street
Jerusalem

Introduction

Jews are truly an international people and their cuisine reflects the countries and regions in which they have lived. Bringing with them their own traditions and customs, they have adapted the ingredients and dishes of these countries and created their own specialities. In some cases the origins of dishes have become lost through transplantation from one country to another. However, two distinct trends are still discernible – the Spanish Sephardim and the European Ashkenazim.

In each country where they have settled, Jews have learned to adapt to the regional foods and climate. In Eastern Europe where the winters were bitterly cold and people were not very wealthy, dishes were adapted so that they were economical, filling and warming and that stretched resources. Thus, we find dishes like Kneidlach and Kreplach, Perogen, Gefilte fish (for which we have vegetarian recipes) and hearty soups like cabbage and beetroot and Krupnik (barley and mushroom). These would be Ashkenazi dishes. The Sephardim (Spanish Jews, originally) and the near Eastern and Middle Eastern Jews have dishes made from the plentiful produce of those regions, such as aubergines and pulses.

Chopped liver and chopped herring, for which there are vegetarian recipes here, feature at many Jewish functions all over the world, although they are European in origin. Galuptzi (Russian stuffed cabbage leaves), Klops (German-Jewish cottage pie), Lechso (Hungarian sautéed peppers, onions and tomatoes) are all examples of Ashkenazi dishes. Avocado soup, now popular in Israel, could have originated in South America. Fritada le Espinaca (spinach soufflé), Mejedra (rice and lentil pilaff), Lahne be Sahem (layered casserole) and Borekas (savoury baked turnovers) are examples of Sephardi dishes. The

9

ubiquitous aubergine features in many Israeli dishes and appears in a number of recipes. Today's shrinking world has brought all the various cultures together in countries like Israel and the United States of America. Many dishes that were once regional have become international.

In Jewish teachings, eating is regarded as a hallowed act, to be accompanied by the recitation of appropriate blessings. Each meal is a reminder of the bountifulness of the earth's produce for which we express our gratitude with blessings and thanksgiving.

In ancient times the Jews were an agricultural people, their lives revolved around the cycle of sowing, reaping and harvesting their crops; praying for the early rains ('yoreh', the heavy rains towards the end of October) and the latter rains ('malkosh', the downpours of March and April), upon which their harvests depended. Closeness to the earth and reliance on its produce brought about an increased awareness of the dependence of human beings on the Almighty. Just as the Sabbath is the pinnacle of each week, the Festivals crown the seasons in which they appear. Jewish life and tradition is bound up with these occasions, which are celebrated in happiness and with thanksgiving to the Almighty. Incorporated within these traditions are the mitzvot (good deeds) of hospitality and charity. The Passover Haggadah (prayer book) opens with the invitation

Let him who is hungry come and eat. Let him who is needy come and celebrate the Passover.

We move from one Festival to the next through the year, renewing our spiritual awareness, extending hospitality to friends and relatives.

The Sabbath

Each week we have the privilege and joy of experiencing the beneficent Sabbath – truly the Queen, the 'Bride', as she is called in the Sabbath hymn. It is said that it is meritorious to think of the Sabbath all week. How does one do this? Any delicacy or delicious fruit one sees in the shops should be purchased with Sabbath in mind so that the best and choicest is kept for this day. In the Western world, where we have so much, it is fitting to remember times when people were poor yet, somehow, still managed to honour the Sabbath.

It is said that each person receives an 'extra soul' on the Sabbath, so that we are doubly able to perceive enjoyment and satisfaction and receive physical and spiritual nourishment from this most special of days. The prayers, the laws, the rituals, the peace and happiness that descends on the whole family are enhanced by the joyful presentation of delicious meals. The world, with all its distractions and demands is effectively shut out.

Sunset on Friday is the time when the Sabbath commences. As no cooking is permitted, all preparations are made in advance and the prepared food is kept warm. The Friday evening meal might consist of mock chopped liver, soup with Lokshen or Perogen, a main course of mock chicken casserole or Klops with Tzimmes, roast potatoes, green vegetables and salads. Fruit compote, or Farfel Apple Tart and Sabra ice-cream might be served. Special, sweet, red wine is present on the Sabbath table, together with the two Challahs (Sabbath loaves). Saturday's lunch might be hot, in which case, Cholent and Knaidel would be eaten. If a cold meal is preferred, it might begin with iced Borsht, egg and onion, mock chopped liver or mock chopped herring, cold slices of Klops, a variety of salads, followed by Russian berry Kissel or Orange Surprise.

The Festivals

Each Festival brings to mind tastes and smells, sounds and sights, the excitement of the preparations, the participation of the children and the anticipation of the arrival of the guests. When we celebrate the Festivals, we are participating in the history of our people.

Passover
Passover is the celebration of our redemption from slavery. It takes place in the spring and was also celebrated as an agricultural harvest festival. An omer (measure) of barley was presented at the Temple in Jerusalem on the second day of Passover. Preparations for this Festival are rigorous. All leaven is banished from the house. Bread is replaced by matzo

11

(unleavened bread) and confectionery is baked with matzo meal, ground hazelnuts, almonds or walnuts and potato flour. Ashkenazim (European Jews) and Sephardim (Spanish and Portuguese Jews) have different customs relating to the consumption of pulses. The Passover recipes given in Chapter 8 do not include pulses, but reflect the variety of dishes that may be prepared with vegetables, fruit, nuts and matzo..

Shavuoth

Summertime sees the celebration of Shavuoth, or, the Feast of Weeks (seven weeks after the second day of Passover). It is also known as Chag HaBikkurim. Not only does it commemorate the Revelation of the Law on Mount Sinai, but it is a celebration of the wheat harvest, which is the last of the grains to ripen, and the commencement of the fruit harvest. In ancient times, on Shavuoth, thanksgiving offerings of bread baked with fine, new flour from the wheat harvest, and offerings of the first ripe fruit were brought to the Temple in Jerusalem. Those who lived near Jerusalem brought fresh figs and grapes, while dried figs and raisins were brought by those living further away. These days, synagogues and houses are decorated with leaves, flowers and plants. Schoolchildren bring attractive baskets of fruit to school, which are then taken to charitable institutions. Cheesecakes, cheese Blintzes, honey and fruit dishes are very popular.

Rosh Hashonah

Rosh Hasonah (The New Year) is celebrated at the beginning of autumn. It is a time for people to consider their actions and behaviour and to pray for forgiveness of their sins and for a good year. Symbolic of sweetness, honey cake, Tzimmes with carrots, honey and apples are eaten during Rosh Hashonah. A newly ripened fruit, not yet tasted that season, is served on the second night of Rosh Hashonah, for which a special benediction is said.

Yom Kippur

Yom Kippur (The Day of Atonement) is the culmination of the Days of Awe, the Ten Days of Penitence that begin with Rosh Hashonah. It is a solemn day of fasting, prayer and repentance. At the conclusion of the Fast, hopeful that their prayers have been heard, family and friends gather together to break their

Fast – some with a full-scale meal, others with a simple and light repast, such as sponge cake and fruit juices. Thoughts are already turning towards the celebration of the next Festival.

Succoth

Succoth (Tabernacles) follows four days after Yom Kippur. It is the third of the three Pilgrim Festivals, the other two being Passover and Shavuoth. Not only is it a harvest festival, but it commemorates the 40 years' wandering in the desert before the entry into the Promised Land.

Temporary booths are erected in gardens, roofed over with leaves and branches, and decorated within with flowers, fruit and pictures of the Holy Land. All meals are eaten in the Succah, as it is called, where starlight and sunlight filter through the branches overhead. Being the end of the fruit harvest, fruit strudels, tarts and fruit salads play a prominent part in the menu.

The seventh, eighth and ninth days of Succoth are known respectively as Hoshana Rabbah, Shemini Atzeret and Simchat Torah (Rejoicing of the Law). This last day is a special favourite with the children who receive presents of nuts and raisins, sweets and chocolates, symbolic of the sweetness of the Law.

Chanukah

Chanukah, or, the Festival of Lights, occurs in December. Latkes (fritters fried in oil) are eaten to remind us of the miracle of the pure oil, of which one day's supply lasted for eight days during the restoration of the Holy Temple.

Purim

Purim, which takes place one month before Passover, is a time for joyful merry-making and the sending of cakes, fruit, wine and so on to friends and relations. It is a perennial reminder of a great deliverance from evil during the reign of Ahasuerus. Kreplach and Hamantaschen are usually eaten on this Festival.

Tu Bi'Shvat

Among the minor festivals, Tu Bi'Shvat celebrates 'the beginning of the season of the budding of the trees' and is also known as 'New Year of the Trees'. A variety of sweet fruits, especially Israeli fruits, such as grapes, raisins, almonds, dates and figs, are eaten.

Rosh Chodesh
Last, but not least, is Rosh Chodesh (New Moon), celebrated in Biblical times as a holiday, but no longer today. Something special, perhaps a favourite hors-d'oeuvre or dessert is added to the meal in honour of the New Moon.

The Jewish vegetarian kitchen

The Orthodox vegetarian family obviously need not have separate sets of dishes, cutlery and utensils for meat and milk. Naturally, however, separate utensils are required for Passover.

There are certain things Jewish vegetarians must pay careful attention to. Only kosher parev margarines should be used, as many others contain animal fats or derivatives. Kosher cheese and jellies should also be used.

All berries, salad greens, fruit and vegetables should be scrutinized and thoroughly washed before use, as it is forbidden to eat even the tiniest insect. Pulses, grains, nuts and flour should be carefully examined for any sign of insect life. Eggs should be checked for blood spots and discarded if any are found.

By presenting delicious and nourishing menus here, we hope to be able to provide you with the inspiration to satisfy family and friends and increase your joy by knowing that vegetarianism and Judaism are in complete harmony.

Some steps towards a healthy life-style

As more and more people are becoming aware of the health benefits of a vegetarian diet, let me share some brief general guidelines to good health from the experts.

Taking regular exercise, breathing good, clean, dry air, and drinking good, clean water are prerequisites for good health. Regular exercise need not be strenuous: brisk walking is good for the circulation, health of your heart, digestion, suppleness, stamina and so on. Take care, though, not to exercise straight after you have eaten or to eat a full meal just before you go to bed.

Eating breakfast every morning should be a regular part of your daily routine as it fuels the body for the morning's activity. Eating slowly and chewing your food well prepares it better for the digestive system. Good, clean water is the best drink of all for the body and drink it cool rather than cold. However, drinking with meals is not recommended.

Excessive over-eating harms the body, distending the organs in the stomach area, and so it is wise not to eat unless you are hungry, nor drink unless you are thirsty. Following this advice also helps to avoid you putting on extra weight.

People who are cheerful and optimistic, who are stable in their emotions and behaviour, who exercise their bodies as well as their minds, eat a balanced diet and do not over-eat are well on their way to good health.

Living your life in this way, using your own good sense and enjoying the healthy, good food you can prepare using the recipes in this book, cannot but be good for you. I wish you healthy and happy eating.

Rose Friedman

Helpful hints and using this book

It is much easier and quicker to have everything ready *before* you start to cook the recipe so simplify things by planning ahead, saving yourself time and effort:

- read the recipes carefully so you can have all the ingredients and equipment ready and know what the method involves
- in some cases, presoaking and cooking of beans or some other form of preparation is required, so do not be caught out (making double quantities when cooking beans and freezing half or having some tinned beans are good ideas).

Beans and lentils

Before cooking dried beans and Continental (brown) lentils, check them carefully (as you should all pulses), removing any little stones, etc. Rinse them well and then leave them to soak in plenty of water, preferably overnight. Rinse them well again and then boil them in fresh water for about 20 minutes. Drain off the cooking water, cover with fresh water and boil again until the beans or lentils are tender. This method makes beans and lentils easier to digest.

The time it takes to cook various types of beans and lentils can vary quite a lot so follow the instructions given on the packaging.

When cooking beans and lentils (except split red lentils, which cook very quickly) it is useful to cook more than you require and to freeze the rest. They freeze well and so it is time-saving and economical to simply cook once and thaw some the next time you need them. Washed and dried plastic margarine or other tubs make useful storage containers, but never put hot food into them. Cool the food quickly by standing the saucepan in a bowl of cold water.

More expensive but very convenient are tins of beans, which can be great time savers.

Breadcrumbs
Make breadcrumbs by grinding bread that is a few days old in a food processor. This makes good breadcrumbs, which can be conveniently stored in a sealed plastic tub in the freezer for some months.

Fresh parsley
After washing and drying fresh parsley, store some in a closed plastic bag in the freezer. Next time you need chopped parsley, simply crumble a frozen sprig or two between your fingers over the dish.

Grated cheese
Grate cheese in advance and store it in a sealed plastic tub in the freezer, ready for when you need it. You can just take out as much as is required for each recipe.

Lemons
Keep fresh lemons handy. The juice, zest or peel are used in so many recipes. A useful thing to know is that if you place lemons in hot water for a few minutes before squeezing, they yield more juice. A squeeze of lemon is a good substitute for a pinch of salt at the table.

Pastry
For strudels, roll the pastry out directly onto silicone or greaseproof paper that has been dusted with flour. You can then simply lift the paper with the pastry to the baking sheet without worrying about the pastry sticking or breaking.

Baking blind
This means to bake a pastry case for 10-15 minutes before adding the filling and returning it to the oven to finish cooking. This ensures that the pastry is crisp.

Put a piece of silicone or greaseproof paper in the unbaked pastry case and fill it with shelled almonds. The almonds will have a delicious roasted flavour and can be eaten as they are or used in other recipes. Many cooks fill their unbaked cases with rice or dried beans, which have to be discarded, or special

17

ceramic baking beans. Using almonds is much more fruitful.

Portions
The recipes in this book serve four to six people, unless otherwise specified.

Measures
When using the recipes, measure out the ingredients using *all* imperial, *all* metric or *all* American measures as the conversions are as close as possible, but cannot be exact and although most recipes will be unaffected by these slight differences, the results of others – particularly cakes and so on – may not be as successful.

❖ 1 ❖
Hors-d'oeuvres

❖ Avocado and Egg ❖

Imperial (Metric)		American
2	ripe avocados	2
4	free-range, hard-boiled/hard-cooked eggs	4
2 tsp	lemon juice	2 tsp
2 tsp	grated/shredded onion	2 tsp
	mayonnaise, for blending	
	sea salt and freshly ground black pepper	

Garnish
chopped fresh parsley

1 Halve the avocados, remove the stone (pit), remove all the flesh from the skins and put it into a bowl.
2 Mash the flesh with a fork.
3 Shell and mash the eggs.
4 Combine the avocado, egg and remaining ingredients, mixing them well to form a soft purée. Chill.
5 Serve chilled and decorated with the parsley. This is delicious on thin slices of wholemeal (whole wheat) bread.

Hummus with Tahini

Imperial (Metric)		American
½ lb (225g)	raw chick peas/garbanzo beans	1 cup
2 tbsp	olive oil	2 tbsp
2	cloves garlic, crushed/minced	2
	juice of 1 lemon	
	sea salt	
4 fl oz (45ml)	tahini (pure sesame paste)	½ cup
	paprika or cayenne pepper	

Garnish
olives, stoned/pitted and halved
sprig parsley

1 Soak the chick peas (garbanzos) in water overnight and then rinse them well. Cook them gently in plenty of water for about 2 hours until they are soft. Drain and mash them well or purée them in a liquidizer or food processor.
2 Combine the chick pea (garbanzo) purée with the olive oil, garlic, lemon juice, salt and tahini and mix them together well to form a smooth paste. If it is too dry, add a little more oil.
3 Sprinkle the paprika or cayenne over and chill. Serve decorated with the olives and parsley. Can be served as a dip with crackers.

Mock Chopped Herring

Imperial (Metric)		American
1	medium aubergine/eggplant	1
1 tbsp	olive oil	1 tbsp
2	thick slices soft wholemeal/whole wheat bread *or* challah	2
4-6 tbsp	cider vinegar	4-6 tbsp
4	free-range eggs, hard-boiled and shells removed	4
1	medium onion, grated/shredded	1
2	large apples, grated/shredded	2
1 tbsp	light demerara sugar, to taste	1 tbsp
	sea salt	
	pinch ground ginger	
	freshly ground black pepper	

Garnish
sprigs of parsley
few slices of cucumber
few slices of tomato

1 Preheat the oven to 475°F/240°C/gas mark 9.
2 Halve the aubergine (eggplant) lengthwise, oil the cut surfaces and place the halves cut side down on a baking sheet in the preheated oven for about 20 minutes until the skin has shrivelled, then leave them to cool a little.
3 When they are cool enough to handle, remove the skin and mash the pulp.
4 Soak the bread in the vinegar and a little water until it is soft and then mash it well.
5 Mash 3 of the eggs finely (reserve the remaining one for decoration).
6 Mince in a liquidizer or food processor or combine by hand all the remaining ingredients together with the aubergine, bread and egg to form a smooth, moist spread.
7 Mash the yolk and white of the reserved egg separately and use them to decorate the paste, garnishing it with the parsley sprigs, slices of cucumber and tomato. This hors-d'oeuvre is often served on festive occasions.

21

Danish 'Hirring' in Sweet and Sour Sauce

Imperial (Metric)		American
1 medium	aubergine (eggplant)	1 medium
1	stick celery, chopped	1
1 small	onion, chopped	1 small
1	Granny Smith apple, chopped	1
	Sauce	
2 fl oz (60ml)	cider vinegar	¼ cup
2 tbsp	sunflower oil	2 tbsp
2 tbsp	water	2 tbsp
2 tsp	sugar	2 tsp
1 tbsp	tomato purée (paste)	1 tbsp
½ tsp	mustard	½ tsp
	sea salt, freshly ground black pepper and paprika	

1 Peel the aubergine (eggplant) and cut the flesh into small strips.
2 Steam or boil it until it is just tender, but not mushy, and drain.
3 Combine the aubergine (eggplant) strips with the celery, onion and apple.
4 Mix the sauce ingredients together very well and pour the sauce over the aubergine (eggplant) mixture and stir it in well.
5 Refrigerate the dish and serve it chilled.
6 Hand round Challah or brown bread as well, which are delicious used to mop up the sauce.

Avocado Vinaigrette

Imperial (Metric)		American
2 large	ripe avocados	2 large
½	lemon	½
1 small	onion, finely chopped	1 small
4 heaped tbsp	finely chopped fresh parsley	4 heaped tbsp
4 tbsp	sunflower oil	4 tbsp
2 tbsp	cider vinegar	2 tbsp
	sea salt and freshly ground black pepper	
1	pickled cucumber, diced	1
a few	lettuce leaves, shredded	a few

1 Cut the avocados in half lengthwise and remove the stones (pits), just before serving.
2 Squeeze the lemon over the avocado flesh to prevent it discolouring.
3 Mix the onion, parsley, oil and vinegar together and season to taste with sea salt and freshly ground black pepper. Spoon the mixture into the cavities in the avocados left by the stones (pits).
4 Sprinkle the pickled cucumber over the mixture.
5 Place each avocado half on a bed of the shredded lettuce.

Note
If the avocados happen to have a bruise or two and do not look attractive, you can still use them. Scoop out the unbruised flesh using a melon baller. Mix together 3 tablespoons mayonnaise and 2 teaspoons tomato purée (paste) with the onion and parsley mixture, then stir it with the avocado balls, coating them with the mixture. Serve in individual glass dishes that have been lined with shredded lettuce.

Mock Fried Fish

Imperial (Metric)		American
1 medium	aubergine (eggplant), peeled	1 medium
	sea salt	
3 oz (85g)	wholemeal (whole wheat) flour	¾ cup
	or matzo meal	
	freshly ground black pepper and paprika	
1 tsp	dried, mixed herbs	1 tsp
1-2	free-range eggs, beaten	1-2
	sunflower oil, for frying	

Garnish
1 lemon, sliced

1   Thinly slice the aubergine (eggplant), layer the slices in a colander or large plate, salting each layer and leave for 30 minutes until the bitter juices have oozed out. Rinse the slices, then pat them dry.
2   Combine the flour or matzo meal with the seasonings, to taste, and the herbs.
3   Dip the aubergine (eggplant) slices first into the seasoned flour or matzo meal, then into the beaten egg and fry in batches in hot oil until they are golden brown on both sides.
4   Drain them on kitchen paper (paper towels).
5   Serve with the lemon slices.

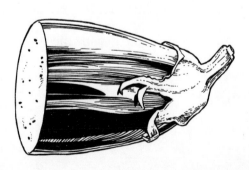

Mock Chopped Liver 1
(Green Beans and Eggs)

Imperial (Metric)		American
1	onion, finely chopped	1
1	stick/stalk celery, finely chopped	1
2 tbsp	polyunsaturated margarine	2 tbsp
2	free-range eggs, hard-boiled and shelled	2
½ lb (225g)	cooked green beans, finely diced	1 cup
½ lb (225g)	peas, cooked	1⅓ cups
½ lb (225g)	English walnut pieces	1⅔ cups
½ tsp	dried oregano	½ tsp
	sea salt and freshly ground black pepper	

Garnish
a few slices of pickled cucumber, olives and
chopped fresh parsley

1 Brown the onion and celery in the margarine.
2 Mash the eggs.
3 Blend together the onion and celery, eggs, green beans, peas, walnuts, oregano and season to taste with sea salt and freshly ground black pepper. Chill.
4 Serve it cold, decorated with the pickled cucumber, olives and parsley.

Mock Chopped Liver II
(Aubergine and Eggs)

Imperial (Metric)		American
1 large	aubergine/eggplant	1 large
3	free-range eggs, hard-boiled/hard-cooked	3
3	medium onions, finely chopped	3
1	clove garlic, crushed/minced	1
	corn oil, for frying	
	sea salt and freshly ground black pepper	
½ tsp	dried mixed herbs	½ tsp
½ tsp	dried oregano	½ tsp

1 Prick the aubergine (eggplant) all over with a fork and put it on a baking sheet in a hot oven 425°F/220°C/gas mark 7 oven and bake it until the skin shrivels and the flesh is soft (about 20-30 minutes).
2 Leave the aubergine (eggplant) to cool, then peel it and mash the flesh.
3 Peel and chop the eggs.
4 Fry the onions and garlic in a little oil, to which a little sea salt and freshly ground black pepper and the herbs have been added.
5 Add the aubergine (eggplant) and cook all the ingredients, except the eggs, together until they have browned.
6 Drain off any excess oil, add the eggs then purée the mixture in a liquidizer or food processor to form a soft pâté.

Baba Ganoush
(Aubergine Dip)

Imperial (Metric)		American
1 large	aubergine (eggplant)	1 large
or 2 small		*or* 2 small
3	cloves garlic, crushed (minced)	3
2 tbsp	chopped fresh parsley	2 tbsp
1 tbsp	lemon juice	1 tbsp
1 tbsp	olive oil	1 tbsp
	sea salt and freshly ground black pepper	
3-4 tbsp	mayonnaise	3-4 tbsp
	Garnish	
a few	green and black olives, stoned (pitted)	a few

1 Preheat the oven to 400°F/200°C/gas mark 6.
2 Prick the aubergine (eggplant) all over with a fork, wrap it in foil and put it on a baking sheet in the preheated oven. Bake it for about 40-50 minutes or until it is soft.
3 Leave it to cool, then slice it open and remove the pulp from the skin (discard the skin).
4 Process the aubergine (eggplant) pulp with the garlic, parsley, lemon juice and olive oil in a liquidizer or food processor and season to taste with sea salt and freshly ground black pepper.
5 Stir in the mayonnaise and check the seasoning, adjusting it if necessary.
6 Refrigerate the dip and serve it chilled, garnished with the green and black olives.

Eier Mit Tzibbale I
(Egg and Onion)

Imperial (Metric)		American
6	free-range eggs, hard-boiled, shelled and finely mashed	6
1 small	onion, grated/shredded	1 small
1	spring onion (scallion), chopped	1
1 tbsp	chopped fresh parsley	1 tbsp
	Sea salt, freshly ground black pepper and garlic salt	
	mayonnaise	
1 tsp	tomato purée/paste	1 tsp

Garnish
a few slices tomato
a few slices cucumber
a few slices radish
sprig parsley

1 Mix the first four ingredients together very well.
2 Add the seasonings to taste and sufficient mayonnaise to bind the mixture to a smooth pâté-like consistency. Mix in the tomato purée.
3 Garnish the mixture with the tomato, cucumber, radish and the parsley. Serve with crackers.

Eier mit Tzimbale II
(Egg and Onion)

Imperial (Metric)		American
3 medium	onions, finely chopped	3 medium
1	clove garlic, chopped	1
6	free-range eggs, hard-boiled (hard-cooked) and roughly chopped	6
	sunflower oil, for frying	
1-2 tsp	sea salt	1-2 tsp
½ tsp	freshly ground black pepper	½ tsp
pinch	ground ginger	pinch
	To serve	
1-in (2.5-cm) piece	cucumber, sliced	1-inch piece
¼ stick	celery, cut into sticks	¼ stalk
1	carrot, cut into sticks	1

1 Sauté the onion and garlic in a little oil until they are golden brown, then turn the heat down to very low and cook very slowly until the onions turn a very deep, caramel brown (about 15-25 minutes).
2 Combine the egg, the onion and garlic mixture, plus the oil in which they were fried, and process the mixture in a liquidizer or food processor. Add the sea salt, freshly ground black pepper and ground ginger and stir them well into the mixture. Check the seasoning and add more to taste if desired. Chill until required.
3 Serve chilled, with the cucumber, celery and carrot sticks for decoration.

Mock Petzah
(Savoury Jelly)

Imperial (Metric)		American
2	pickled cucumbers, sliced	2
3	olives, stoned	3
1-2	tomatoes, sliced	1-2
1-2	carrots, cut into sticks/strips	1-2
3-4	free-range eggs hard boiled (hard-cooked) (optional)	3-4
About ¾ lb (340g)	mixture of cooked vegetables (peas, green beans, potatoes, carrots, mushrooms marinated for 30 minutes in lemon juice and mayonnaise, asparagus tips, etc.)	About 2 cups
2½ pts (1.5 l)	water	6¼ cups
	juice of 2 large lemons	
1	vegetable stock (bouillon) cube	1
1	clove garlic, crushed (minced)	1
1 oz (30g)	fresh parsley, chopped	1 cup
1 tsp	caraway seeds	1 tsp
1 tsp	mixed dried herbs	1 tsp
3½ tsps	agar agar	3½ tsps

1 Arrange the vegetables as attractively as possible in a wetted jelly mould or glass dish. Slices of egg, if using may be arranged over the bottom and sides of the mould with slices of pickled cucumber, olives and tomato and carrot sticks in between. Put the cooked vegetables and mushrooms on top.
2 Now prepare the jelly. Boil 2 pints (1.1 litre/5 cups) of the water with the lemon juice, stock (bouillon) cube, garlic, parsley, caraway seeds and herbs for about 30 minutes.
3 Boil the rest of the water in a separate pan and add the agar agar to it, stirring very quickly until it dissolves. Remove it from the heat.
4 Add the agar agar mixture to the stock mixture and simmer gently (do not let it boil) for 3 minutes.
5 Pour the mixture over the prepared vegetables in the mould.
6 Leave it to cool, then chill overnight until it has set completely. Turn out and decorate before serving with

piped mayonnaise stars, or avocado mashed with lemon juice, or asparagus spears, olives or whatever as desired.

❖ ────────────────────────────── ❖

Tsavay
(Yogurt or Sour Cream with Vegetables)

Imperial (Metric)		**American**
⅔ pt (340ml)	natural (unsweetened) yogurt	1½ cups
	or sour (soured) cream	
¾ lb (340g)	mixture of vegetables	2 cups

(tomatoes, cucumbers, celery, grated/shredded carrots,
spring onions (scallions), fresh shredded spinach,
cooked or fresh beetroot, radishes,
green pepper), chopped
sea salt
freshly ground black pepper

Garnishes
a few carrot sticks
a few slices cucumber
a few wedges tomato
a few sprigs parsley
a few lettuce leaves

1 Combine all the ingredients in a glass bowl and decorate it with the carrot sticks, radish and cucumber slices, tomato wedges and parsley.
2 Serve it on plates lined with lettuce leaves.

Variation
For a light lunch, add cottage (pot) cheese, and serve with wholemeal bread or Pumpernickel.

Red Peppers with Yogurt

Imperial (Metric)		American
2 large	red peppers, deseeded and chopped	2 large
2-3 tbsp	olive oil, for frying	2-3 tbsp
1 tbsp	finely chopped, fresh parsley	1 tbsp
1 small	spring onion (scallion), finely chopped	1 small
⅓ pt (200ml)	natural (unsweetened) yogurt	¾ cup
	sea salt and freshly ground black pepper	
pinch	paprika	pinch

1 Fry the red pepper in the olive oil until it is soft.
2 Combine the pepper well with the rest of the ingredients and chill until you are ready to serve. Then season to taste with sea salt and freshly ground black pepper and sprinkle the paprika over it.

Avocado Dip

Imperial (Metric)		American
2 medium	ripe avocados	2 medium
2-3 tbsp	lemon juice	2-3 tbsp
¼	stick celery, finely chopped	¼
1	tomato, peeled and chopped	1
1	spring onion (scallion), chopped	1
1-in (2.5-cm) piece	fresh cucumber, finely chopped	1-inch piece
	sea salt and freshly ground black pepper	
3-4 tbsp	mayonnaise	3-4 tbsp
	Garnishes	
2 tsp	chopped fresh parsley	2 tsp
8	olives, stoned (pitted)	8
1	carrot, cut into sticks	1
¼ stick	celery, cut into sticks	¼ stalk

1 Halve the avocados, remove the stone (pit) and carefully remove all the flesh.
2 Mash the avocado flesh with the lemon juice.
3 Mix in the remaining ingredients, combining everything well together (add more mayonnaise if a creamier texture is required). Chill.
4 Serve chilled, garnished with the parsley, olives and carrot and celery sticks or as desired.

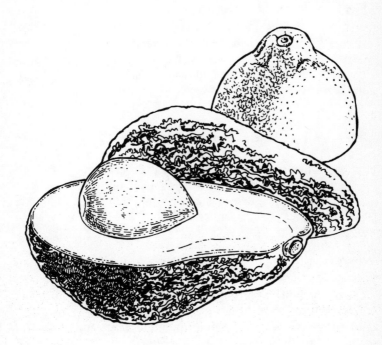

'Hirring' Vorspeis
(Mock Herring Appetizer)

Imperial (Metric)		American
1 medium	aubergine (eggplant)	1 medium
3	beetroot (beets), steamed or boiled and chopped	3
2	potatoes, steamed or boiled and chopped	2
1	pickled cucumber, chopped	1
1	Granny Smith apple, chopped	1
1 small	onion, finely chopped	1 small
½	stick celery, finely chopped	½
2 tbsp	cider vinegar	2 tbsp
1 tbsp	sunflower oil	1 tbsp
1 tsp	light demerara sugar	1 tsp
1-2 tsp	sea salt	1-2 tsp
¼ tsp	freshly ground black pepper	¼ tsp
½ pt (285ml)	natural (unsweetened) yogurt	1⅓ cups
	Garnishes	
1 tbsp	finely chopped fresh parsley	1 tbsp
1 tbsp	finely chopped fresh chives	1 tbsp
2	free-range eggs, hard-boiled (hard-cooked) and cut into quarters (optional)	2
½	red pepper, deseeded and cut into thin strips	½
a few	lettuce leaves	a few

1　Peel the aubergine (eggplant) and cut the flesh into small strips.
2　Steam or boil the strips until they are just tender, but not mushy, then drain them.
3　Mix together with the remaining ingredients and chill until you are ready to serve.
4　Serve garnished with the parsley, chives, egg, if using, and red pepper serving it onto plates lined with lettuce leaves.

❖ 2 ❖
Soups and
Soup Accompaniments

Note: Vary the thickness of your soups according to your preference, by adding more or less water according to taste. British cups are 10 fl oz (285ml); American cups are 8 fl oz.

❖ Clear Vegetable Soup ❖

Imperial (Metric)		American
6-8 cups	water	6-8 cups
2	carrots, grated (shredded)	2
2	onions, sliced	2
2	tomatoes, sliced	2
2 sticks	celery, chopped	2 stalks
1 oz (30g)	chopped fresh parsley (including stems)	1 cup
1	potato, chopped	1
1	clove garlic, chopped	1
	sea salt and freshly ground black pepper	
½-1 tsp	dried mixed herbs	½-1 tsp
2	vegetable stock (bouillon) cubes (optional)	2
1 tsp	yeast extract *or* soya sauce	1 tsp

1 Bring the water to the boil, then add all the other ingredients and simmer, covered, for about 1 hour.
2 Strain out the vegetables and adjust the seasoning, if necessary. Purée the strained vegetables in a liquidizer or food processor and return to the pot, mixing them in well.
3 Serve the soup hot with Kreplach, Perogen, Mandalach, Kneidlach (see page 50–3).

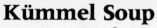

Kümmel Soup
(Caraway Seed Soup)

Imperial (Metric)		American
7-8 tsp	caraway seeds	7-8 tsp
4 cups	water	4 cups
2 tbsp	rolled oats	2 tbsp
1	free-range egg	1
2 tsp	wholemeal (whole wheat) flour	2 tsp
	sea salt and freshly ground black pepper	
1	vegetable stock (bouillon) cube	1

1 Boil the caraway seeds in the water and then simmer for about 1½ hours, replacing the water that evaporates.
2 Strain the caraway seeds from the liquid, reserving ½ teaspoon of the caraway seeds, then return the liquid and the ½ teaspoon of caraway seeds to the pan and heat.
3 Add the rolled oats and simmer for about 15-20 minutes.
4 Beat the egg lightly and mix the flour with it to form a smooth liquid (it should not be too thick). Mix in a little sea salt and freshly ground black pepper.
5 Bring the soup to the boil and drop the egg mixture in a teaspoon at a time. Let it cook through, mixing it in well as it does so.
6 Serve hot.

Gemüse Soup
(Vegetable Soup)

Imperial (Metric)		American
2	carrots, grated (shredded)	2
1	potato, grated (shredded)	1
2	onions, grated (shredded) or chopped	2
2	celery sticks (stalks), chopped	2
	vegetable oil, for frying	
6-8 cups	water	6-8 cups
2	courgettes (zucchini), chopped	2
1	ripe tomato, skinned and chopped	1
5 oz (140g)	brown rice	½ cup
2 oz (55g)	split red lentils	⅓ cup
1 tsp	dried mixed herbs	1 tsp
2	vegetable stock (bouillon) cubes	2
	sea salt and freshly ground black pepper	

1 Lightly fry the carrot, potato, onion and celery in a little oil in a saucepan for about 5 minutes.
2 Add the water and bring to the boil.
3 Add the courgette (zucchini), tomato, rice, lentils and herbs.
4 Simmer for about 1 hour, or until the vegetables are tender.
5 Crumble the stock (bouillon) cubes into the soup and simmer for about another 10 minutes.
6 Season to taste with sea salt and freshly ground black pepper.

Note
Leftover soup may be frozen and, when thawed, made into a different soup by adding fresh peas, cooked butter (lima) beans, barley, macaroni or whatever you wish.

Mushroom Soup

Imperial (Metric)		American
1 medium	onion, finely chopped	1 medium
1 medium	carrot, grated (shredded)	1 medium
1	stick celery, finely chopped	1
	sunflower oil, for frying	
¾ lb (340g)	mushrooms, chopped	¾ lb
6 cups	vegetable stock	6 cups
1 tsp	soy sauce (soya sauce)	1 tsp
	sea salt and freshly ground black pepper	
2 tbsp	dry sherry (dry sherry wine) (optional)	2 tbsp
	Garnish	
1-2 tsp	chopped fresh parsley	1-2 tsp

1 Sauté the onion, carrot and celery in a little oil in a saucepan until the onion begins to soften. Add the mushrooms, stirring, and cook gently for about 10-15 minutes until the mushrooms are soft.
2 Add the vegetable stock, soy sauce and season to taste with sea salt and freshly ground black pepper. Simmer for about 30 minutes, then add the sherry, if using.
3 Serve hot, garnished with a fine sprinkling of the parsley over each bowlful.

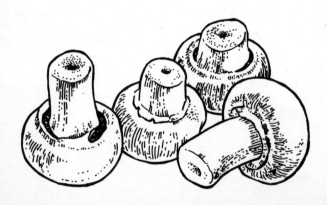

Hobernergroten Soup
(Oat and Vegetable Soup)

Imperial (Metric)		American
2 medium	carrots, grated (shredded)	2 medium
1 large	onion, chopped	1 large
1 stick	celery, chopped	1 stalk
1	parsnip, grated (shredded)	1
1	potato, grated (shredded)	1
2 tbsp	vegetable oil	2 tbsp
2	vegetable stock (bouillon) cubes	2
6-8 cups	water	6-8 cups
4 oz (115g)	*hoobergrits* (oats)	½ cup
	sea salt and freshly ground black pepper	
1 tsp	dried mixed herbs	1 tsp
2 tbsp	chopped fresh parsley	2 tbsp

1 Fry the vegetables in the oil until they are soft but not brown.
2 Crumble in the vegetable stock (bouillon) cubes, add the water and bring to the boil.
3 Rinse the *hoobergrits* (oats) well under running water through a sieve (strainer) and add them to the soup. Season to taste with sea salt and freshly ground black pepper, then stir in the herbs.
4 Simmer the soup gently for about 1 hour, until the vegetables are tender.
5 Taste and adjust the seasoning if necessary, then serve hot.

Onion and Tomato Soup

Imperial (Metric)		American
2 large	Spanish onions (Bermuda onions), finely chopped	2 large
2	cloves garlic, chopped	2
	sunflower oil, for frying	
4 ripe	tomatoes, chopped	4 ripe
1 tbsp	tomato purée (paste)	1 tbsp
1 tbsp	chopped fresh parsley	1 tbsp
1 tsp	dried mixed herbs	1 tsp
	sea salt, freshly ground black pepper and paprika	
6 cups	vegetable stock	6 cups
2 tbsp	raw fine noodles	2 tbsp

1 Sauté the onion and garlic in a little oil in a saucepan until they are golden brown and have softened. Add the tomatoes and simmer the mixture gently for about 10-15 minutes. Then, stir in the tomato purée, herbs and season to taste with sea salt and freshly ground black pepper.
2 Add the stock and noodles, bring the soup to the boil and simmer for about 30-45 minutes.

Bean and Barley Soup

Imperial (Metric)		American
6 oz (170g)	butter (lima) beans (soaked overnight)	1 cup
2	carrots, grated (shredded)	2
1	onion, chopped	1
1	potato, chopped	1
2 tbsp	oil	2 tbsp
6-8 cups	water	6-8 cups
5 oz (140g)	barley, well rinsed	½ cup
1	tomato, peeled and chopped	1
	sea salt and freshly ground black pepper	

1 Boil the butter (lima) beans until they are tender.
2 Gently sauté the carrot, onion and potato in the oil until they are tender.
3 Add the water, the cooked butter (lima) beans, the barley, tomato and season to taste with sea salt and freshly ground black pepper.
4 Bring the soup to the boil and then simmer for about 1-1½ hours, covered, stirring from time to time.

Split Pea and Barley Soup

Imperial (Metric)		American
2	carrots, grated (shredded)	2
1	onion, chopped	1
1 stick	celery, chopped	1 stalk
2 tbsp	vegetable oil	2 tbsp
6-8 cups	water	6-8 cups
1 tbsp	chopped fresh parsley	1 tbsp
2	vegetable stock (bouillon) cubes (optional)	2
½ lb (225g)	split peas (soaked overnight)	1 cup
5 oz (140g)	barley, well rinsed	½ cup
	sea salt and freshly ground black pepper	

1 Fry the carrot, onion and celery in the oil until they are tender.
2 Add the water, parsley, stock (bouillon) cubes, if using, the split peas and barley and bring to the boil. Simmer for about 1 hour until the peas and barley are tender. Season to taste with sea salt and freshly ground black pepper and stir in a little more water if the consistency has become too thick.

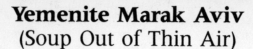

Yemenite Marak Aviv
(Soup Out of Thin Air)

Imperial (Metric)		American
1 tbsp	cumin seeds	1 tbsp
1 tbsp	black peppercorns	1 tbsp
1 tbsp	cardamom pods	1 tbsp
2 tbsp	turmeric seeds	2 tbsp
1 tsp	whole cloves	1 tsp
6 cups	water	6 cups
2	free-range eggs	2

1 First make a Chawaijh by grinding together all the spices to a powder in a mortar or coffee grinder.
2 Bring the water to the boil in a saucepan and add 1 tablespoon of the Chawaijh (store the rest in an airtight spice jar for another time).
3 Beat the eggs very well.
4 Dribble the beaten eggs slowly into the boiling soup mixture so that it cooks as it enters the hot soup, forming fine threads.
5 Boil the soup for 10 more minutes.
6 Serve with pitta bread.

Kartoffel Soup
(Potato Soup)

Imperial (Metric)		American
1	onion, chopped	1
1 oz (30g)	polyunsaturated margarine	2½ tbps
1	carrot, grated (shredded)	1
1 stick	celery, chopped	1 stalk
3	potatoes, peeled and chopped	3
3 cups	water	3 cups
3 cups	milk	3 cups
	sea salt and freshly ground black pepper	
2 tbsp	chopped fresh parsley	2 tbsp
	Garnish	
4-6 tbsp	sour (soured) cream *or* natural (unsweetened) yogurt (optional)	4-6 tbsp

1 Brown the onion in the margarine in a saucepan.
2 Add the carrot, celery, potato, water and milk and bring to the boil. Season to taste with sea salt and freshly ground black pepper and simmer for about 30 minutes, or until the vegetables are tender.
3 Add the parsley and simmer for a further 10 minutes. Serve garnished with the sour cream or yogurt, if desired.

Krupnik
(Barley and Mushroom Soup)

Imperial (Metric)		American
2 tbsp	polyunsaturated margarine	2½ tbsp
2	carrots, finely grated (shredded)	2
1 medium	onion, finely chopped	1 medium
2 oz (55g)	mushrooms, chopped	¾ cup
6-8 cups	water	6-8 cups
2	vegetable stock (bouillon) cubes	2
10 oz (285g)	barley	1¼ cups
	sea salt and freshly ground black pepper	
	Garnish	
1 tbsp	chopped fresh parsley (optional)	1 tbsp

1 Melt the margarine in a saucepan and gently fry the carrot, onion and mushrooms until they have softened (about 15 minutes).
2 Add the water and the stock (bouillon) cubes and bring to the boil.
3 Add the barley and the seasonings, bring to the boil and simmer for about 1-1½ hours, stirring from time to time (add some water if the consistency becomes too thick).
4 Serve the soup hot, garnished with the parsley, if using.

Marak Avocado
(Avocado Summer Soup)

Imperial (Metric)		American
2 medium-sized	ripe avocados	2 medium-sized
	juice of ½ lemon	
4-5 cups	vegetable stock	4-5 cups
	sea salt and freshly ground black pepper	
	Garnish	
4-6 slices	lemon	4-6 slices

1 Cut the avocados in half lengthwise, remove the stones (pits) and scoop out the flesh into a liquidizer or food processor.
2 Purée the avocado pulp (mash it or push it through a sieve if you do not have a liquidizer or food processor).
3 Combine the avocado purée with the remaining ingredients, blending them well together.
4 Chill the soup until you are ready to serve and serve it cold. (This soup may also be served hot, in which case heat it up, but do not let it boil.) A little dry white wine may be added.) Garnish each bowlful with a slice of lemon, floating it on the surface.

 # Cabbage Borsht

Imperial (Metric)		American
1 large	beetroot (beet), peeled and chopped	1 large
1 large	onion, chopped	1 large
2	carrots, grated (shredded)	2
¼ small	white cabbage, thinly sliced	¼ small
2 tbsp	polyunsaturated margarine	2 tbsp
6-8 cups	water	6-8 cups
2	tomatoes, skinned and chopped	2
2	potatoes, peeled and diced	2
	sea salt and freshly ground black pepper	
	Garnish	
4-6 tbsp	sour (soured) cream *or* natural (unsweetened) yogurt	4-6 tbsp

1 Put the beetroot (beet), onion, carrot and cabbage into a saucepan and add the margarine.
2 Add the water and bring it to the boil.
3 Add the tomato and potato and season to taste with sea salt and freshly ground black pepper and simmer for about 1-1½ hours.
4 Serve the soup hot, garnished with the sour cream or yogurt.

Sweet and Sour Cabbage and Apple Soup

Imperial (Metric)		American
⅓ pt (200ml)	tomato juice	¾ cup
2	vegetable stock (bouillon) cubes	2
6-8 cups	water	6-8 cups
½ small	white cabbage, finely chopped	½ small
2 large	cooking (tart) apples, chopped	2 large
1 medium	onion, grated (shredded)	1 medium
	sea salt and freshly ground black pepper	
	juice of 1 lemon	
	honey, to taste	

1 Boil together the tomato juice, vegetable stock (bouillon) cubes and water.
2 Add the cabbage, apple and onion to the boiling mixture, reduce the heat and simmer for 1-2 hours until the cabbage is tender.
3 Season to taste with sea salt and freshly ground black pepper, add the lemon juice and a tesapoon or so of honey to taste for a sweet-sour flavour, then serve hot.

Beetroot Soup
(Cold or Hot)

Imperial (Metric)		American
4-6 large	beetroot (beet)	4-6 large
6-8 cups	vegetable stock	6-8 cups
	sea salt and freshly ground black pepper	
	juice of 1 lemon	
	honey, to taste (optional)	

1 Wash and peel the beetroot (beet).
2 Simmer them in a saucepan in the stock, for about 1½-2

hours, until they are tender. Strain off the cooking liquid and
return it to the pan.

3 Grate (shred) the beetroot (beet) when they are cool enough
to handle, and return to the pan (or, if a clear soup is
preferred, reserve for a salad). Cook the soup for 10 minutes.

4 Season to taste with sea salt, freshly ground black pepper,
the lemon juice and honey, if using, leave to cool, then chill
until you are ready to serve.

5 Serve it as it is, garnished with chopped cucumbers and a
spoonful of cream or mix it with an equal quantity of milk
and top each bowl with a spoonful of sour cream or yogurt
or serve the soup with a hot, boiled potato in each bowlful.

Schav
(Summer Sorrel Soup, Served Cold)

Imperial (Metric)		American
1 lb (455g)	sorrel *or* spinach	1 lb
6-8 cups	water *or* vegetable stock	6-8 cups
	juice of 1 lemon	
	sea salt and freshly ground black pepper	
2 tsp	sugar	2 tsp
	Garnish	
4-6 tbsp	cream *or* natural (unsweetened) yogurt	4-6 tbsp
handful	watercress leaves	handful

1 Wash the sorrel or spinach leaves very thoroughly, cut them
up roughly and boil them in the water for about 20-30
minutes.

2 Purée the soup in a liquidizer or food processor.

3 Add the lemon juice, season to taste with sea salt and freshly
ground black pepper and the sugar.

4 Let the soup cool then chill it until you are ready to serve.
Serve it cold, with a spoonful of the cream or yogurt and
decorate with the watercress leaves.

47

Peach or Plum Summer Soup

Imperial (Metric)		American
8 ripe	peaches *or* 12 ripe sweet plums	8 ripe
4-6 cups	water	4-6 cups
	demerara sugar, to taste	
2 tsp	lemon juice	2 tsp
	Garnish	
4-6 tbsp	cream *or* natural (unsweetened) yogurt	4-6 tbsp

1 Boil the peaches or plums in the water until they are soft.
2 Lift the fruit from the pan, remove the stones (pits) and purée the fruit in a liquidizer or food processor.
3 Return the purée to the pan.
4 Add the sugar to taste.
5 Leave to cool then chill until you are ready to serve. Serve with the cream or yogurt.

Galia Soup

Imperial (Metric)		American
1 large	ripe Galia or other melon	1 large
½ pt (285ml)	orange juice	1⅓ cups
1 tbsp	lemon juice	1 tbsp
¼ tsp	ground cinnamon	¼ tsp
¼ tsp	ground ginger	¼ tsp
⅓ pt (200ml)	white wine *or* apple juice	¾ cup
	Garnish	
10-12	strawberries, halved	10-12

1 Halve the melon, remove the seeds and scoop out the flesh.
2 Liquidize the melon with the orange juice, lemon juice and spices.

3 Stir in the white wine or apple juice and chill until you are ready to serve.
4 Serve chilled, garnished with the strawberries.

Cold Fruit Soup

Imperial (Metric)		American
1 lb (455g)	assorted fruits (berries, cherries, apricots, pears, plums, peaches)	3 cups
6 cups	water	6 cups
2 tsp	lemon juice	2 tsp
¼ tsp	ground cinnamon	¼ tsp
1-2 tsp	honey	1-2 tsp
	sweet red wine (optional)	
	Garnish	
4-6 tbsp	sour (soured) cream *or* natural (unsweetened) yogurt	4-6 tbsp

1 Slice the larger fruit and remove the stones (pits), but do not peel them.
2 To the water in a saucepan, add the lemon juice, cinnamon, honey and the wine, if using.
3 Simmer all the fruit in this liquid until it is soft.
4 Purée the fruit in a liquidizer or food processor, then return it to the saucepan.
5 Simmer it for a short while, then leave it to cool and chill it until you are ready to serve. Serve it cold with the cream or yogurt.

Mandalach
(Soup Nuts)

Imperial (Metric)		American
½ tsp	sea salt	½ tsp
About 6 oz (170g)	self-raising brown/wholewheat flour	About 1½ cups
2	free-range eggs, lightly beaten	2
1 tbsp	corn oil	1 tbsp

1 Preheat the oven to 375°F/190°C/gas mark 5.
2 Stir the sea salt into the flour, then make a well in the middle.
3 Add the eggs and oil, pouring them into the well and mix to make a soft, firm dough. Add a little more flour if the dough is too sticky.
4 Knead the dough well and roll it out into long ropes. Cut these into tiny pieces about the size of half an almond.
5 Spread the pieces on a well-greased baking sheet and bake them in the preheated oven for about 15-20 minutes or until they are golden brown.
6 Serve Mandalach with clear soups or green pea soup or use them as croûtons.
7 Store unused Mandalach in a closed jar for several weeks.

Perogen
(Savoury Filled Pasties)

Makes 12-14

Imperial (Metric)		American
½ lb (225g)	self-raising brown/wholewheat flour	2 cups
2 tsp	baking powder	2 tsp
	sea salt and freshly ground black pepper	
	onion salt	
	garlic salt	
1	free-range egg, lightly beaten	1
2 fl oz (60ml)	corn oil	¼ cup
3-4 tbsp	water, to mix	3-4 tbsp
1 × recipe	filling (see note)	1 × recipe
1	free-range egg, beaten or water to glaze	1
	sesame seeds	

1 Preheat the oven to 375°F/190°C/gas mark 5.
2 Mix together the flour, baking powder and a pinch of the seasonings and make a well in the middle of the mixture.
3 Pour into the well the egg and corn oil and mix them in well to form a dough. Add the water gradually until you have a soft dough.
4 Knead the dough and then divide it into small pieces and roll these out very thinly (when they are rolled out, each piece should measure approximately 4×4 inches/ 10×10cm).
5 Place a heaped tablespoon of your chosen filling in the centre of the square, then moisten your fingers with water and pinch the edges of the dough closed over the filling.
6 Brush the Perogen with the beaten egg or water and sprinkle a few sesame seeds over, then bake them in the preheated oven for about 25 minutes or until they are golden brown.
7 Serve the Perogen in Clear Vegetable Soup (see page 35) or hot Beetroot (Beet) Soup (see page 37).

Note

For the filling, use the Klops I (see page 58) or Klops III (see page 60) recipes, adding a little water or vegetable stock to moisten the filling. A mashed hard-boiled free-range egg may also be added to the filling.

Also, if you have any leftover Perogen, they make a delicious light meal served with vegetables.

Kneidlach
(Soup Dumplings)

Makes about 12

Imperial (Metric)		American
2	free-range eggs	2
4 fl oz (115ml)	water	½ cup
2 tbsp	corn oil	2 tbsp
	sea salt and freshly ground black pepper	
2 tsp	ground cinnamon	2 tsp
4 oz (115g)	Matzo meal	1 cup

1   Beat the eggs very well until they are light and frothy.
2   Add the water and the oil and beat them well again.
3   Season to taste with sea salt, freshly ground black pepper and ground cinnamon, and gradually add the matzo meal until the mixture is of a soft consistency, like oatmeal porridge.
4   Chill the mixture for about 1 hour.
5   Have a large pot of boiling, salted water on the stove when the hour is up and form the Kneidlach mixture into small balls. Drop the balls into the gently boiling water and cook them for about 20 minutes. Allow plenty of room for expansion as they almost double in size. They are traditionally served in clear soup on Friday nights and Festivals.

Kreplach
(Small Savoury-filled Dough Pockets)

Makes about 24

Imperial (Metric)		American
¼-½ tsp	sea salt	¼-½ tsp
½ lb (225g)	self-raising brown/wholewheat flour	2 cups
3	free-range eggs	3
1 tbsp	water	1 tbsp
½ × recipe	filling (see note)	½ × recipe

1 Mix the salt into the flour, then make a well in the middle. Beat the eggs slightly and pour them into the well in the flour.
2 Add the water and knead the ingredients into a stiff dough.
3 Roll the dough out thinly on a floured surface then cut it into small squares measuring 2½-3 inches (6.5-7.5cm).
4 Place a heaped teaspoonful of your chosen filling on the centre of each square.
5 Moisten your fingertips with water and seal the squares to form small triangles.
6 Drop the Kreplach into boiling, salted water and remove them with a slotted spoon after about 15 minutes.
7 Serve them hot in clear soup.

Note
For the filling, use Lentil Klops I (see page 58) or Klops III (see page 60), adding a little water or vegetable stock to moisten the filling.

Also, any leftover Kreplach are very good with Mushroom Sauce (see page 94) and cheese.

❖ 3 ❖
Main Courses

❖ Couscous with Chick Peas and Vegetables ❖

Imperial (Metric)		American
½ lb (225g)	quick cooking couscous	1½ cups
8 fl oz (240ml)	cold water	1 cup
1 small	aubergine/eggplant	1 small
	sea salt and freshly ground black pepper	
2 medium	onions, cut into chunks	2 medium
2	cloves garlic, crushed/minced	2
2 medium	potatoes, peeled and cut into large pieces	2 medium
2	courgettes/zucchini, cut into chunks	2
1	carrot, cut into chunks	1
2	ripe tomatoes, peeled and chopped	2
1	stick celery, chopped	1
	piece of pumpkin (optional)	
1 lb (455g)	tinned/canned chick peas/ garbanzo beans, drained	1 lb
	sunflower oil, for frying	
1½-2 pt (850-1100ml)	boiling water	4-5 cups
1 tsp	turmeric	1 tsp
½ tsp	cayenne	½ tsp
½ tsp	pepper	½ tsp
½ tsp	fenugreek	½ tsp
1 tsp	ground cumin	1 tsp
2	vegetable stock (bouillon) cubes	2

1 Put the couscous in a large bowl and sprinkle the cold water over it to dampen it, or prepare it according to the directions, on the packet.
2 Cut the aubergine (eggplant) into slices and layer them in a colander or large plate, sprinkling sea salt over each layer and leave them to stand for 30 minutes, or until the bitter juices have oozed out, then rinse the slices and pat them dry.
3 Fry the vegetables in large saucepan in some oil for about 10 minutes.
4 Add the boiling water, spices and seasonings and stock (bouillon) cubes and simmer for about 20 minutes. Then add the chick peas (garbanzos).
5 Put the damp couscous into a large strainer and set this over the saucepan. Cover the pan with a cloth and the lid so that the couscous steams over the simmering vegetables until the couscous is tender (see the directions on the packet for how long this should take).
6 To serve, spoon the couscous around the edges of a large serving dish. Using a slotted spoon, heap the vegetables in to centre of the serving dish.
7 Hand the strained cooking liquid around separately for people to ladle over their plates as they wish.

Note
This is usually prepared in a special couscoussier. The strainer is an improvization.

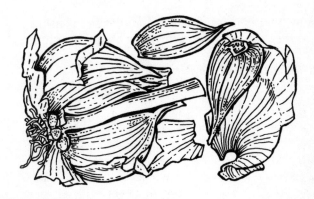

Cashew Nut Casserole
(Mock Chicken Casserole)

Imperial (Metric)		American
3oz (85g)	polyunsaturated margarine	⅓ cup
1½oz (45g)	wholemeal/whole wheat flour	6 tbsp
1 tsp	sea salt	1 tsp
	freshly ground black pepper	
⅔ pt (340ml)	vegetable stock	1½ cups
8 fl oz (240ml)	milk *or* soya milk	1 cup
3 oz (85g)	mushrooms, chopped	1 cup
1 tbsp	chopped onion	1 tbsp
	vegetable oil, for sautéing	
5 oz (140g)	cashew nuts	1 cup
2 oz (55g)	black olives, stoned/pitted and sliced	½ cup
2 tbsp	white wine (optional)	2 tbsp

1 Melt the margarine in a saucepan and stir in the flour and sea salt and freshly ground black pepper to taste.
2 Remove the pan from the heat and slowly blend in the vegetable stock and the milk.
3 Return the pan to the heat and bring to the boil, stirring all the time.
4 Sauté the mushrooms and onions in a little oil and add them to the sauce.
5 Add the cashew nuts, olives and wine, if using.
6 Simmer the casserole gently for about 20 minutes, stirring occasionally.
7 Serve it hot with brown rice and a green salad.

Mock Salmon Rissoles

Imperial (Metric)		American
1 medium	onion, chopped	1 medium
	sunflower oil, for frying	
2	slices fresh wholemeal/whole wheat bread	2
1 lb (455g)	tinned/canned chick peas/garbanzo beans, drained	1 lb
3 tbsp	tomato purée/paste	3 tbsp
3 tbsp	chopped fresh parsley	3 tbsp
	sea salt, freshly ground black pepper and paprika	

1 Sauté the onion in a little oil until it is golden brown.
2 Crumble the bread over the onion in the pan and let it soak up the oil and juices from the onion.
3 Add the chick peas/garbanzos, the tomato purée/paste, parsley and season to taste with sea salt, freshly ground black pepper and paprika.
4 Mash everything together by hand or in a liquidizer or food processor. The mixture should not be too smooth, but should be firm enough to form into rissoles.
5 Preheat the oven to 350°F/180°C/gas mark 4.
6 Moisten your hands and form tablespoons of the mixture into rissoles.
7 Place them on a baking sheet lined with baking parchment, flattening them slightly. Put about ½-1 teaspoon of oil on each rissole.
8 Bake them for about 30 minutes or until they have cooked through and become crisp on the outsides.
9 Serve them hot with sautéed or mashed potatoes, tomato sauce and green vegetables or cold with salads.

Note
A quick tomato sauce can be made by sautéing a little onion, adding chopped/tinned or ripe, peeled tomatoes, chopped parsley, seasoning and a little water or stock and cooking them until the tomatoes are mushy and the sauce is flavourful.

Klops I
(Savoury Casserole)

Imperial (Metric)		American
½ lb (225g)	brown lentils, soaked overnight and well rinsed	1 cup
1 pt (570ml)	water *or* vegetable stock	2½ cups
2 medium	onions, sliced	2 medium
2	cloves garlic, crushed/minced	2
1 medium	carrot, grated/shredded	1 medium
2 tbsp	corn oil	2 tbsp
3 oz (85g)	mushrooms, chopped	1 cup
1 tsp	yeast extract *or* soya sauce	1 tsp
1 tbsp	tomato purée/paste	1 tbsp
1 tbsp	chopped fresh parsley	1 tbsp
2 tbsp	wheatgerm	2 tbsp
	sea salt and freshly ground black pepper	
	chilli powder *or* cayenne pepper	
2 fl oz (60ml)	vegetable stock	¼ cup
1 tbsp	lemon juice	1 tbsp
1 oz (30g)	cheese, grated/shredded	¼ cup
3 oz (85g)	fresh wholemeal/ whole wheat breadcrumbs	1 cup

1 Bring the soaked lentils to the boil in the water or vegetable stock and simmer until they are tender (about 30 minutes).
2 Sauté the onions, garlic and carrot in the oil until they have softened (about 15 minutes).
3 Add the mushrooms and cook for a further 10 minutes.
4 Preheat the oven to 375°F/190°C/gas mark 5.
5 Mash the cooked lentils with a potato/vegetable masher or purée them in a liquidizer or food processor. The mixture should not be too smooth.
6 Combine the lentil purée, the onion, garlic, carrot and mushroom mixture and the remaining ingredients together well, except for the lemon juice, cheese and breadcrumbs. Spoon the mixture into a well-greased casserole dish and sprinkle the lemon juice over it.
7 Bake in the preheated oven for about 45 minutes. Sprinkle

the cheese and breadcrumbs over the top about 20 minutes before the end of this cooking time, when the topping should be bubbling and golden brown.

Klops II
(Savoury Casserole)

Imperial (Metric)		American
4 oz (115g)	mixed nuts, finely chopped (cashews, hazelnuts/filberts, walnuts)	1 cup
1 large	onion, finely grated/shredded	1 large
1 oz (30g)	fresh wholemeal/whole wheat breadcrumbs	½ cup
2	free-range eggs	2
1 tbsp	chopped fresh parsley	1 tbsp
	sea salt and freshly ground black pepper	
1 tbsp	yeast extract *or* soy/soya sauce	1 tbsp
¾ pt (425ml)	tomato juice	2 cups

1 Preheat the oven to 350°F/180°C/gas mark 4.
2 Put all the ingredients, except the tomato juice, into a bowl and mix them together well.
3 Spoon the mixture into a greased casserole dish and pour the tomato juice over the top.
4 Bake in the preheated oven for 45-60 minutes (cover the casserole halfway through if it seems to be drying out).
5 Serve with brown rice, vegetables and salads or cold, in slices, with salads and mayonnaise.

Note
You can decorate this dish by lining the bottom and sides of the casserole dish with onion rings, courgette/zucchini slices and celery sticks, before placing the mixture into the casserole.

A topping may be made by sautéing finely chopped or puréed mushrooms with 1 finely chopped or puréed onion and spreading the mixture over the Klops mixture before baking it in the oven.

Klops III
(Savoury Casserole)

Imperial (Metric)		American
1 medium	onion, finely chopped	1 medium
1	clove garlic, crushed/minced	1
2 tbsp	sunflower oil	2 tbsp
4 oz (115g)	Tvp soya mince (soya grits), rehydrated as directed on packet/package	1 cup
3 or 4 medium	ripe tomatoes, peeled and chopped	3 or 4 medium
1	carrot, grated/shredded	1
2 tbsp	chopped fresh parsley	2 tbsp
1 oz (30g)	fresh wholemeal/whole wheat breadcrumbs or	½ cup
2 oz (55g)	cooked brown rice	⅓ cup
1 tbsp	yeast extract or soy/soya sauce	1 tbsp
2 tsp	dried mixed herbs	2 tsp
1 tsp	paprika	1 tsp
1	free-range egg (optional)	1
	vegetable stock, hot	
3 or 4	parboiled potatoes, for topping	3 or 4
1 tbsp	polyunsaturated margarine	1 tbsp
1-2 tbsp	lemon juice	1-2 tbsp
	freshly ground black pepper	

1 Sauté the onion and garlic in the oil until they have softened.
2 Add the tomatoes to the pan.
3 Combine the remaining ingredients, except the last four, in a bowl and add a sufficient vegetable stock to moisten and soften the mixture.
4 Spoon it into a well-greased casserole dish and pour over a little hot vegetable stock (about ½ pt/285ml/1⅓ cups).
5 Preheat the oven to 350°F/180°C/gas mark 4.
6 Slice the potatoes thinly and place them in overlapping rings to cover the mixture completely. Dot with the margarine, and sprinkle lemon juice and freshly ground black pepper over the top.
7 Bake in the preheated oven for about 45 minutes, or until the potatoes are crispy and golden brown on top.

Note

The toppings may be varied: you can mash the potatoes instead of slicing them, mixing in a little milk, salt and pepper, and spread it over the Klops; steamed, puréed cauliflower, blended with a little milk and flour, seasoned with nutmeg and topped with grated/shredded cheese is delicious spread on top of the Klops.

Arroz Asapado
(Chick Pea and Rice Casserole)

Imperial (Metric)		American
½ lb (225g)	chick peas/garbanzo beans	1 cup
2 large	onions, finely chopped	2 large
2	cloves garlic, crushed/minced	2
2 fl oz (60ml)	vegetable oil	¼ cup
2 large	ripe tomatoes, skinned and chopped	2 large
	sea salt and freshly ground black pepper	
1⅓ pt (770ml)	hot vegetable stock	3¼ cups
½ lb (225g)	brown rice	1 cup

1 Soak the chick peas (garbanzo beans) in cold water and keep them in the refrigerator for 24 hours. Rinse them thoroughly, then bring them to the boil for 10 minutes, rinse them again and simmer them in fresh water until they are soft (about 2-3 hours simmering).
2 Gently fry the onions and garlic in the oil until golden brown.
3 Add the tomatoes and season to taste with sea salt and freshly ground black pepper and simmer for about 5 minutes.
4 Add the hot stock, rice and cooked chick peas (garbanzo beans).
5 Bring the stock to the boil, then turn down the heat and simmer for about 30 minutes until the liquid has been absorbed and the rice is cooked through.
6 Serve it hot with accompanying vegetables of your choice.

Variation

For extra interest, add 2-3 oz (55-85g/1 cup) fresh mushrooms and a few tablespoons of chopped green pepper, fried with the onions and garlic.

Seniyeh
(Casserole with Sesame Seeds)

Imperial (Metric)		American
½ lb (225g)	green lentils	1 cup
1 large *or* 2 medium	onions, finely chopped	1 large *or* 2 medium
2	cloves garlic, crushed/minced	2
	sunflower oil, for frying	
1 medium	carrot, grated/shredded	1 medium
1	stick celery, finely chopped	1
2 tbsp	finely chopped, fresh parsley	2 tbsp
1 tbsp	tomato purée (paste)	1 tbsp
2 tsp	yeast extract *or* soy sauce	2 tsp
¼ tsp	ground cinnamon	¼ tsp
	sea salt, freshly ground black pepper and paprika	

	Topping	
4 oz (115g)	sesame seeds, lightly toasted	¾ cup
3 fl oz (90ml)	water	⅓ cup
1	clove garlic	1
	juice of 1 lemon	
½ tsp	salt	½ tsp
2 tbsp	pine nuts *or* chopped almonds, lightly toasted in oil	2 tbsp

1 Rinse the lentils well and boil them in plenty of water until they are soft and mushy (about 1 hour). Drain off any excess water.
2 Meanwhile, sauté the onion, garlic, carrot and celery until the onions are golden brown and the carrot is softening.
3 Combine the lentils with the onion mixture, adding the remaining ingredients at the same time and mixing them all well together.
4 Spoon the mixture into a greased, ovenproof casserole dish.
5 Preheat the oven to 375°F/190°C/gas mark 5.
6 Now make the topping. Process the sesame seeds, water, garlic, lemon juice and salt in a liquidizer or food processor.

7 Pour this evenly over the top of the lentil mixture already in the casserole dish.
8 Sprinkle the pine nuts or almonds over the sesame mixture.
9 Bake in the preheated oven for 30-40 minutes or until the mixture is cooked through and the topping has begun to brown.
10 Serve it hot with brown rice.

Hint
Make double the quantity of the lentil mixture and freeze half of it to use another time.

 ——————————————————————

Lechso
(Hungarian Pepper and Tomato Omelette)

Imperial (Metric)		American
1	onion, chopped	1
2 tbsp	sunflower oil	2 tbsp
2-3	red and green peppers, deseeded and chopped	2-3
½ lb (225g)	ripe tomatoes, skinned and chopped	½ lb
2 tsp	paprika	2 tsp
	sea salt and freshly ground black pepper	
4	free-range eggs, beaten	4

1 Sauté the onion in the oil until it has softened and is transparent.
2 Add the peppers and tomatoes and sprinkle the paprika and sea salt and freshly ground black pepper over them. Cook until the peppers are soft.
3 Pour the eggs over the vegetable mixture, stir continuously until the eggs are cooked through, then serve immediately.

❖ ─────────────────────────────────── ❖

Koklaten I
(Lentil Rissoles)

Imperial (Metric)		American
½ lb (225g)	brown lentils, soaked overnight, and rinsed well	1 cup
1 pt (570ml)	water *or* vegetable stock	2½ cups
2 medium	onions, chopped	2 medium
2 tbsp	corn oil	2 tbsp
2	cloves garlic, sliced or crushed/minced	2
3 oz (85g)	mushrooms, chopped	1 cup
1 tbsp	yeast extract *or* soy/soya sauce	1 tbsp
1 tbsp	chopped fresh parsley	1 tbsp
	sea salt and freshly ground black pepper	
	chilli powder *or* cayenne pepper	
2 oz (55g)	fresh wholemeal/whole wheat breadcrumbs	1 cup
2 tbsp	wheatgerm	2 tbsp
1	free-range egg	1
	polyunsaturated margarine	
½	lemon	½

1 Bring the lentils to the boil in the water or vegetable stock and simmer until they are tender (about 30 minutes).
2 Sauté the onions in the oil, add the garlic and fry gently for another 10 minutes.
3 Add the mushrooms, cook for 10 more minutes, then remove the pan from the heat.
4 Mash the cooked lentils with a potato/vegetable masher or in a liquidizer or food processor. The mixture should not be too smooth.
5 Combine the lentil purée with the mushroom and onion mixture, the yeast extract, parsley, seasoning, breadcrumbs, wheatgerm and egg.
6 Preheat the oven to 375°F/190°C/gas mark 5.
7 Shape the mixture into rissoles and place them on a greased baking sheet. Dot each rissole with a little margarine and a squeeze of lemon.
8 Bake them in the preheated oven for about 30 minutes,

making sure that they do not become dry, adding more margarine if necessary.
9 Serve with tomato or mushroom sauce and vegetables of your choice.

Lahne be Sahem
(Layered Casserole)

Imperial (Metric)		American
4 oz (115g)	Tvp soya mince/soya protein grits	1 cup
1 tbsp	tomato purée/paste	1 tbsp
1 tsp	yeast extract *or* soy/soya sauce	1 tsp
3 large	onions, sliced	3 large
1	clove garlic, crushed/minced	1
1 large	green pepper, sliced and deseeded (optional)	1 large
3 tbsp	sunflower oil	3 tbsp
4-5	ripe tomatoes, sliced	4-5
6	parboiled potatoes, sliced	6
	juice of 1 lemon	
2 tbsp	chopped fresh parsley	2 tbsp
	sea salt and freshly ground black pepper	

1 Rehydrate the Tvp soya mince/grits according to the directions on the packet, then add the tomato purée and yeast extract or soy sauce and mix them in well.
2 Lightly fry the onions, garlic and green pepper in the oil until they have softened.
3 Drain the vegetables, reserving the oil.
4 Preheat the oven to 350°F/180°C/gas mark 4.
5 Arrange alternating layers of the fried vegetable mixture, the tomatoes, potatoes and Tvp mince in an ovenproof casserole dish.
6 Combine the reserved oil with the lemon juice, parsley and a little sea salt and freshly ground black pepper. Pour this over the layered vegetables, plus a little hot water.
7 Bake in the preheated oven for about 30-40 minutes.

Variation
Substitute cooked, mashed lentils for the Tvp soya mince/grits.

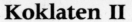

Koklaten II
(Vegetable Rissoles)

Imperial (Metric)		American
2 medium	onions, finely chopped	2 medium
1 large	stick/stalk celery, finely chopped	1 large
2 medium	carrots, finely grated/shredded	2 medium
2 tbsp	corn oil	2 tbsp
6 oz (170g)	peas, cooked	1 cup
6 oz (170g)	French/green beans, cooked	1 cup
1-2	free-range eggs, beaten (optional)	1-2
1 tsp	dried mixed herbs	1 tsp
1 tbsp	yeast extract *or* soy/soya sauce	1 tbsp
1 tbsp	tomato purée/paste	1 tbsp
2 oz (55g)	fresh wholemeal/whole wheat breadcrumbs	1 cup
	sea salt and freshly ground black pepper	
1½ tbsp	polyunsaturated margarine *or* corn oil	1½ tbsp
	seasoned flour (optional)	
1 tbsp	lemon juice	1 tbsp

1 Gently fry the onions, celery and carrots in the oil until they have softened.
2 Combine this mixture with the remaining ingredients, except the seasoned flour, margarine and lemon juice, and mix them together very well. Mash or purée the mixture in a liquidizer or food processor, but should not be too smooth.
3 Chill it for about 30 minutes.
4 Preheat the oven to 350°F/180°C/gas mark 4.
5 Then, form the mixture into rissoles and coat these lightly in the seasoned flour, if using.
6 Place them on a greased baking sheet, dot each rissole with a little of the margarine or a few drops of oil and drizzle a little lemon juice over them.
7 Bake in the preheated oven for 30-40 minutes, then serve with tomato or mushroom sauce, baked potatoes and salads.

Variation
Add ½ a chopped sautéed green pepper, about 6 oz (170g/1 cup) cooked sweetcorn and 1 tbsp soy sauce.

Baked Gefilte Dish

Imperial (Metric)		American
½ lb (225g)	butter (lima) beans, soaked overnight	1½ cups
1	bay leaf	1
small bunch	parsley	small bunch
2	cloves garlic, 1 sliced, 1 chopped	2
1	carrot, sliced	1
2	onions, finely chopped	2
2 oz (55g)	polyunsaturated margarine	¼ cup
3 tbsp	sunflower oil	3 tbsp
1 small	green pepper, chopped	1 small
2	free-range eggs, beaten	2
3 fl oz (90ml)	vegetable stock	⅓ cup
	sea salt and freshly ground black pepper	
2 tbsp	lemon juice	2 tbsp
1½ tbsp	polyunsaturated margarine	1½ tbsp
	Garnish	
1	carrot, cooked and sliced	1

1 Rinse the beans, then boil them fiercely in plenty of water for 10 minutes. Pour off the water, fill the pan with fresh water, bring it to the boil, then simmer with the bay leaf, parsley, the garlic slices and the carrot until they are tender.
2 Drain the beans, discarding the bay leaf and parsley, but reserving the carrot.
3 Sauté the onion in the margarine and oil for a few mintues.
4 Add the green pepper and chopped garlic to the onion and sauté them for 10-15 minutes until the onion and green pepper have softened and are well cooked.
5 Preheat the oven to 350°F/180°C/gas mark 4.
6 Add the beans and mash them well with the onion and pepper, either by hand with a potato/vegetable masher or in a liquidizer or food processor.
7 Add the eggs, season to taste with sea salt and freshly ground black pepper and mix them in well.
8 Spoon the mixture into a greased ovenproof casserole dish, then pour the vegetable stock and lemon juice over it and

dot the top with the margarine.

9 Bake in the preheated oven for about 30 minutes.

10 Garnish with the carrot slices and serve either warm or cold with chrain (horseradish) as a main course or as an hors-d'oeuvre.

Gemüse Kugel
(Rainbow Vegetable Kugel)

Imperial (Metric)		American
3 medium	carrots, grated	3 medium
1 small	cauliflower, broken into florets	1 small
3 medium	potatoes, peeled and chopped	3 medium
6 oz (170g)	peas	1 cup
1	onion, grated/shredded	1
1 large	courgette/zucchini, grated/shredded	1 large
2 sticks	celery, finely chopped	2 stalks
1	ripe tomato, skinned and chopped	1
2 oz (55g)	polyunsaturated margarine	¼ cup
	sea salt and freshly ground black pepper	
2 tbsp	sour milk	2 tbsp
2	free-range eggs, beaten	2
1 tbsp	curd/cottage cheese, mashed	1 tbsp
2 oz (55g)	Gouda cheese, grated/shredded	½ cup
1 oz (30g)	grated/shredded nuts or sesame seeds (optional)	2 tbsp

1 Steam the carrot, cauliflower, potatoes and green peas separately until they are tender.

2 Meanwhile, sauté the onion, courgette/zucchini, celery and tomato in the margarine. Season to taste with sea salt and freshly ground black pepper.

3 Grease an ovenproof dish and preheat the oven to 350°F/180°C/gas mark 4.

4 Mash the carrot and stir in the sour milk, sea salt and freshly ground black pepper and a little of the beaten egg to form a soft consistency. Press it into the bottom of the dish in an even layer.

5   Mash the cauliflower and stir in the curd cheese, plus 1
    tablespoon of the Gouda cheese, sea salt and freshly ground
    black pepper and a little of the beaten egg. Press it on top
    of the carrot mixture in the dish in an even layer.
6   Mash the peas, add a little beaten egg and seasoning and
    press it on top of the cauliflower in an even layer.
7   Mash the potatoes, add 1 tablespoon of the cheese and a
    little of the egg, season and press the mixture on top of the
    peas in an even layer.
8   Spoon the onion, courgette/zucchini, celery and tomato
    mixture evenly over the top, sprinkle the remainder of the
    cheese and the nuts or sesame seeds, if using, over the top
    and bake in the preheated oven for 30 minutes until the top
    is golden brown.

Note
The top may be decorated with carrot strips, dipped in beaten
egg, arranged in a lattice pattern with sliced steamed Brussels
sprouts in each little square.

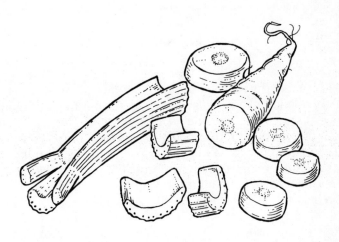

Artichoke Quiche

Imperial (Metric)		American
	Pastry	
2 oz (55g)	butter *or* margarine	¼ cup
4 oz (115g)	self-raising brown/wholewheat flour	1 cup
½ tsp	dried mixed herbs	½ tsp
	sea salt and freshly ground black pepper	
3 tbsp	milk	3 tbsp
	Filling	
14-oz (397-g) tin	artichoke hearts	14-oz can
	(about 8-10) drained, rinsed and diced	
8-10	stoned/pitted green olives, chopped	8-10
1	ripe tomato, skinned and chopped	1
2 tsp	lemon juice	2 tsp
	sea salt and freshly ground black pepper	
½ tsp	fresh *or* dried mixed herbs	½ tsp
2	free-range eggs	2
½ tsp	paprika	½ tsp
⅓ pt (200ml)	single/light cream *or* milk	¾ cup
	Garnish	
6-8	olives, sliced	6-8

1 First, make the pastry. Cut the butter or margarine into the flour, blending it with a pastry cutter or your fingertips until the mixture looks like fine breadcrumbs. Add the herbs, sea salt and freshly ground black pepper and blend them in. Then add the milk, a little at a time, kneading it in lightly until a smooth ball of dough is formed, wrap it in plastic film (plastic wrap) and chill it for 30 minutes.

2 Preheat the oven to 400°F/200°C/gas mark 6.

3 Roll it out, then press it into a greased 8 by 10-inch (20 by 25-cm) pie dish, prick it with a fork and bake it blind (see page 17) in the preheated oven for 10-15 minutes. Turn the oven down to 350°F/180°C/gas mark 4.

4 Now make the filling. Combine the artichoke hearts, olives

and tomato. Add the lemon juice, season to taste with sea salt, and freshly ground black pepper and add the mixed herbs, stirring them in.

5　Spoon the filling into the pastry case (shell).

6　Beat the eggs and cream or milk together and pour the mixture over the vegetable filling in the pastry case (shell).

7　Sprinkle the paprika over the top of the quiche.

8　Bake it for about 20-30 minutes, or until the mixture is firm.

9　Garnish the top with the slices of olive and serve the quiche either hot or at room temperature.

 ———————————————————————

Gemüse Torte mit Kaese
(Vegetable and Cheese Pie)

Imperial (Metric)		American
	Pastry	
2 oz (55g)	polyunsaturated margarine	¼ cup
4 oz (115g)	wholemeal/whole wheat flour	1 cup
1	free-range egg yolk *or* 4 tbsp water	1
	sea salt	
	Filling	
1	aubergine/eggplant	1
	sea salt and freshly ground black pepper	
2	onions, chopped	2
3	courgettes/zucchini, finely chopped	3
3	large tomatoes, skinned and chopped	3
1 small	green pepper, diced	1 small
1	clove garlic, crushed/minced	1
2 oz (55g)	Gouda cheese, grated/shredded	½ cup
1 × 11½ oz (325g) tin	sweetcorn	1 × 11½-oz can
2 tbsp	corn oil, plus extra if required	2 tbsp

1　First, make the pastry. Rub the margarine into the flour until the mixture resembles fine breadcrumbs.

2　Add the egg yolk or water and knead it in slightly until the dough is fairly stiff.

3　Roll the pastry out and line a greased pie dish.

4 Now make the filling. Peel and slice the aubergine (eggplant), lay the slices in a colander or large plate, salting each layer and leave for 30 minutes or until the bitter juices have been drawn out.
5 Meanwhile, sauté the onions, courgettes/zucchini, tomatoes, green pepper and garlic.
6 Rinse the aubergine/eggplant slices, pat them dry, add them to the onion mixture and sauté until they have softened. Season to taste with sea salt and freshly ground black pepper.
7 Preheat the oven to 350°F/180°C/gas mark 4.
8 Sprinkle the pie crust with a third of the cheese and spoon in half the vegetable mixture, including half the sweetcorn. Sprinkle another third of the cheese over the mixture.
9 Spoon in the rest of the vegetable mixture, including the remainder of the sweetcorn, and sprinkle the rest of the cheese on top.
10 Bake in the preheated oven for about 30-40 minutes.

 ———————————————————————

Sweet and Sour Medley

Imperial (Metric)		American
1 large	aubergine/eggplant, sliced	1 large
	sea salt and freshly ground black pepper	
1 large	onion, cut into rings	1 large
1 medium	green pepper, deseeded and chopped	1 medium
2 oz (55g)	button mushrooms, halved	1 cup
	sunflower oil, for frying	
3	ripe tomatoes, chopped	3
1	Golden Delicious apple, peeled and chopped	1
½ lb (225g)	tinned/canned pineapple pieces,	½ lb
	drained, reserving the juice	
1 tbsp	wholemeal/whole wheat flour	1 tbsp
⅓ pt (200ml)	pineapple and apple juice	¾ cup
	mixed together	
2 fl oz (60ml)	wine vinegar	¼ cup
1½ tbsp	honey	1½ tbsp

1 Lay the aubergine (eggplant) slices in a colander or large plate, salting each layer and leave for 30 minutes or until the bitter juices have been drawn out. Rinse them well and pat them dry.
2 Fry the onion rings, green pepper and mushrooms in the oil for about 10 minutes or until the onions have softened and are golden brown.
3 Remove the vegetables from the oil and transfer them to an ovenproof casserole dish.
4 Lightly fry the aubergine (eggplant) slices on both sides in a little oil, then lay them on top of the onion mixture in the casserole dish.
5 Add the tomato, apple and pineapple and season to taste with sea salt and freshly ground black pepper.
6 Preheat the oven to 350°F/180°C/gas mark 4.
7 Blend the flour with some of the juice to make a smooth paste. Bring the rest of the juice to the boil, together with the wine vinegar and the honey. Add some of the hot liquid to the paste, stirring well, add a little more hot liquid, then pour the floury liquid into the hot liquid on the stove. Bring it to the boil again, stirring all the time until it thickens a little.
8 Pour this over the vegetables in the casserole.
9 Bake for 30-40 minutes and serve it with brown rice and salads.

Asparagus Pie

Imperial (Metric)		American
	Pastry	
4 oz (115g)	self-raising brown/wholewheat flour	1 cup
2 tsp	baking powder	2 tsp
	sea salt	
2 oz (55g)	polyunsaturated margarine	¼ cup
2 fl oz (60ml)	milk, or as required	¼ cup
	Filling	
2 tbsp	polyunsaturated margarine	2 tbsp
2 medium	onions, finely chopped	2 medium
2 × ½lb (225g)	tins/cans asparagus pieces	2 × ½lb (225g)
2	free-range eggs	2
¼ pt (140ml)	cream *or* milk	⅔ cup
	freshly ground black pepper	
2 oz (55g)	Gouda cheese, grated/shredded	½ cup
	paprika	

1 First make the pastry. Mix all the dry ingredients together, then rub (cut) the margarine into the flour until it looks like fine breadcrumbs.
2 Add sufficient milk to form a firm dough. Roll the pastry out and line a greased ovenproof pie dish measuring about 8 by 10 inches (20 by 25cm).
3 For the filling, melt the margarine and sauté the onions until they are transparent and have softened. Layer the sautéed onions in the bottom of the pie.
4 Drain the asparagus and spread the pieces over the onions.
5 Preheat the oven to 425°F/220°C/gas mark 7.
6 Beat the eggs until they are light and frothy.
7 Beat the cream, if using, until it is thick.
8 Fold the egg into the cream or milk, season to taste with freshly ground black pepper and pour the mixture over the asparagus. Sprinkle the cheese and a little paprika over the top.
9 Bake for approximately 20-30 minutes until the pie is golden brown. Serve with spinach and salads.

Harshouf Mimuleh
(Stuffed Artichokes)

Imperial (Metric)		American
4 large	globe artichokes	4 large
5 tbsp	lemon juice	5 tbsp
1 medium	onion, finely chopped	1 medium
	sunflower oil, for frying	
1	ripe tomato, skinned and diced	1
1 oz (30g)	fresh wholemeal/whole wheat breadcrumbs	½ cup
½ lb (225g)	tin/can chickpeas/garbanzo beans	1½ cups
	sea salt and freshly ground black pepper	
1 tbsp	tomato purée/paste	1 tbsp
1 tbsp	chopped fresh parsley	1 tbsp
	Garnishes	
1	tomato, sliced	1
10-12	olives, stoned (pitted) and sliced	10-12

1 Prepare the artichokes by washing them well. Cut the stem as close to the base as possible with a sharp knife and twist off the stem so that the artichoke stands upright. Cut the top half of the artichoke away, also with a sharp knife.
2 Boil them in plenty of water to which 2 tablespoons of the lemon juice has been added. Cook them for about 30 minutes or, until when pulled off, the base of a leaf is tender enough to eat.
3 Drain the artichokes, then pull out the leaves from the middle, reserving them for garnishing. Scoop out the hairy chokes with a spoon and rinse the artichokes out well.
4 Preheat the oven to 350°F/180°C/gas mark 4.
5 While the artichokes are cooking, prepare the filling. Fry the onion in a little oil until it is golden brown. Add the diced tomato, breadcrumbs and chick peas (garbanzos). Mash them together well, season to taste with sea salt and freshly ground black pepper, add the tomato purée, 1 tablespoon of the lemon juice and the parsley, combining everything

well. Fill the artichokes with the mixture.

6 Place them in an ovenproof casserole dish and pour hot water in until it is halfway up the sides of the artichokes. Add the rest of the lemon juice and a little sea salt and freshly ground black pepper.

7 Bake them in the preheated oven for about 30 minutes, basting the filling with the hot water once or twice to prevent it drying out.

8 Lift the artichokes out onto a serving plate and garnish them with the tomato, olives and reserved centre leaves. Serve with mayonnaise, to dip the soft edible parts of the leaves into.

 ────────────────────────────

Blinis

Imperial (Metric)		American
	Batter	
2	free-range eggs	2
6 oz (170g)	self-raising brown/wholewheat flour	1½ cups
	sea salt and freshly ground black pepper	
⅔ pt (340ml)	water	1½ cups
	margarine *or* oil, for greasing	

Filling

Sautéed, chopped onions and mushrooms (cooking juices reserved) *or* mashed, tinned/canned, drained asparagus pieces (liquid reserved) *or* cooked, drained, seasoned spinach mixed with curd (farmer's) cheese.

	Sauce	
2 tbsp	polyunsaturated margarine	2 tbsp
1½ oz (15g)	wholemeal/whole wheat flour	2 tbsp
⅓ pt (200ml)	milk	¾ cup
	liquid from tinned/canned asparagus *or* from sautéed mushrooms	
2 oz (55g)	cheese, grated/shredded	½ cup
	freshly ground black pepper	

1 First, make the batter. Beat the eggs until they are frothy.
2 Add the flour, a little sea salt and freshly ground black pepper and, gradually add the rest of the flour and some of the water.
3 Add the rest of the water, gradually, beating each addition in well. The batter should be smooth.
4 Grease an omelette or frying pan (skillet) lightly with margarine or vegetable oil.
5 Pour in about a tablespoon of the batter and swirl the pan (skillet) to distribute the batter evenly. Cook it until the edges lift up easily. Stack the Blinis on a cloth.
6 Roll up the Blinis around some filling, folding them like envelopes.
7 Preheat the oven to 350°F/180°C/gas mark 4.
8 Now make the sauce. Melt the margarine and stir in the flour to make a roux, cooking the flour a little.
9 Blend in the milk and liquid gradually, stirring constantly over a medium heat until the sauce thickens.
10 Arrange the filled Blinis in a greased casserole dish, pour the sauce over them and sprinkle the cheese and freshly ground black pepper over the top.
11 Bake them in the preheated oven for about 15 minutes to heat the Blinis through and melt the cheese.

Mediterranean Casserole

Imperial (Metric)		American
1 medium	aubergine/eggplant	1 medium
	sea salt, freshly ground black pepper and paprika	
	wholemeal/whole wheat flour, as required	
1	free-range egg	1
	sunflower oil, for frying	
4 oz (115g)	button mushrooms, washed and halved	2 cups
1 pt (570ml)	vegetable stock, hot	2½ cups
2-3 tbsp	sweet red wine	2-3 tbsp
14-oz (397-g)	tin/can artichoke hearts (8-10), drained	14-oz
2 tbsp	lemon juice	2 tbsp
	Garnish	
2 tsp	chopped fresh parsley	2 tsp

1 Slice the aubergine (eggplant), lay the slices in a colander or large plate, salting each layer, leave for 30 minutes or until the bitter juices have been drawn out, then rinse and pat them dry.
2 Season about 2-3 tablespoons of flour with sea salt, freshly ground black pepper and paprika.
3 Beat the egg and put it in a little bowl.
4 Dip the aubergine (eggplant) slices into the beaten egg, then into the flour, and fry them for a few minutes in hot oil on both sides until they are lightly golden brown.
5 Arrange the fried slices in an ovenproof casserole dish.
6 Heat about 1 tablespoon of fresh oil, in the pan and lightly fry the mushrooms.
7 Drain the mushrooms by lifting them out of the pan using a slotted spoon and transfer them to the casserole dish, putting them on top of the aubergine (eggplant).
8 Add 1½-2 tablespoons of flour to the oil in the pan in which the mushrooms were fried, mixing it in to form a smooth paste. Slowly add the hot vegetable stock, with the pan still on the heat, stirring constantly until you have a thick sauce. Add the wine to the sauce, stirring well, and remove the pan

from the heat. Season it to taste with sea salt, freshly ground black pepper and paprika.

9 Preheat the oven to 350°F/180°C/gas mark 4.

10 Arrange the artichoke hearts in the casserole dish and sprinkle the lemon juice over them.

11 Pour the sauce over the vegetables in the casserole dish.

12 Bake the casserole in the preheated oven for about 30 minutes. Sprinkle the fresh parsley over the dish just before you serve.

13 Serve it hot with brown rice, lemon wedges and bread fingers fried in oil into which a garlic clove has been crushed (minced).

Spinach and Cheese Strudel

Imperial (Metric)		American
	Pastry	
6 oz (170g)	wholemeal/whole wheat flour	1½ cups
2 tbsp	Gouda cheese, grated/shredded	2 tbsp
½ tsp	dried mixed herbs	½ tsp
4 oz (115g)	polyunsaturated margarine	½ cup
¼ pt (140ml)	cold water	⅔ cup
1 tsp	lemon juice	1 tsp
	Filling	
2	onions, finely chopped	2
1	clove garlic, crushed/minced	1
2 oz (55g)	polyunsaturated margarine	¼ cup
2	tomatoes, finely chopped	2
2 tbsp	chopped fresh parsley	2 tbsp
	sea salt and freshly ground black pepper	
1 tsp	paprika	1 tsp
1	free-range egg, beaten	1
½ lb (225g)	curd cheese	1 cup
2 oz (55g)	Gouda cheese, grated/shredded	½ cup
1 tbsp	tomato purée/paste	1 tbsp
1 lb (450g)	frozen cooked spinach, defrosted, chopped and drained	2 cups

1 First make the pastry. Mix together the flour, cheese and herbs and cut the margarine in and then rub it in until the mixture resembles fine breadcrumbs.

2 Add the water, gradually, and the lemon juice and combine everything well to form a soft dough. Add a little flour if the dough is too sticky.

3 Roll the dough out into a rectangular shape and fold it over twice, press the edges down, turn to the left. Do this twice more and then chill the dough until required.

4 Now make the filling. Sauté the onions and garlic in the margarine until they are golden brown and then add the tomatoes, parsley and season to taste with sea salt and freshly ground black pepper and the paprika. Gently cook the mixture for a few more minutes then remove the pan from heat.

5 Reserving a little of the beaten egg for brushing the pastry, mix together the egg, cheeses, tomato purée and the spinach, then combine this mixture with the sautéed onion and tomato mixture.

6 Preheat the oven to 400°F/200°C/gas mark 6.

7 Remove the pastry from the refrigerator and divide it into 4 pieces. Roll each piece out into a rectangular shape on floured silicone paper.

8 Divide the filling between the 4 pastry shapes, spreading it evenly and leaving a good margin around the edges. Roll each up to form rolls and put them on a greased baking sheet.

9 Brush them with the reserved egg and a little water and oil mixed together. Bake them for about 30 minutes or until they are golden brown.

Hint
Prepare the strudels on silicone paper, then lift the paper on to the baking sheet and you will be sure that they will not stick.

Mock Seafood Mayonnaise

Imperial (Metric)		American
½ lb (225g)	butter/lima beans, soaked overnight	1½ cups
1	bay leaf	1
1	clove garlic, sliced	1
small bunch	parsley	small bunch
	sea salt, freshly ground black pepper and paprika	
1-2	fresh carrots, grated/shredded	1-2
3 tbsp	mayonnaise	3 tbsp
2 tbsp	tomato purée/paste	2 tbsp
1 tbsp	cider vinegar	1 tbsp
2 tbsp	lemon juice	2 tbsp
	Garnishes	
a few	lettuce leaves	a few
1-2	free-range eggs, hard-boiled (hard-cooked) and sliced	1-2
½	stick celery, cut into sticks	½
2	carrots, cut into sticks	2
8-10	olives	8-10
2	tomatoes, cut into wedges	2

1 Rinse the beans, then put them into a pan with plenty of water, bring to the boil and boil fiercely for 10 minutes. Drain the beans, fill the pan with fresh water, bring it to the boil, then simmer the beans with the bay leaf, garlic and parsley until the beans are tender. Remove the bay leaf and the parsley.
2 Drain the beans and mash them with a potato (vegetable) masher (do not purée them in a liquidizer or food processor as the mixture should not be too smooth). Add a little water if the mixture is too dry.
3 Season the bean mash to taste with sea salt, freshly ground black pepper and paprika.
4 Mix the carrot into the bean mixture.
5 Combine the mayonnaise, tomato purée, vinegar and lemon juice and mix this into bean and carrot mixture.
6 Chill it until required and then serve sprinkled with paprika on the lettuce leaves, with the celery, carrot, egg, olives and tomato.

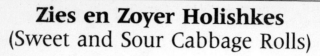

Zies en Zoyer Holishkes
(Sweet and Sour Cabbage Rolls)

Imperial (Metric)		American
1 medium	cabbage	1 medium
1 medium	potato, grated/shredded	1 medium
	1 × Klops recipe (see page 58)	
¾ pt (425ml)	vegetable stock, hot	2 cups
2 medium	onions, grated/shredded	2 medium
3	ripe tomatoes, skinned and chopped	3
6	stoned/pitted prunes, cut into quarters	6
	sea salt and freshly ground black pepper	
	juice of 1 medium lemon	
1½ tbsp	honey	1½ tbsp

1 Put the cabbage in a pan of boiling, salted water for about 5 minutes — just long enough to soften leaves.
2 When it is cool enough to handle, separate the leaves and wash them carefully under running, cold water.
3 Mix the potato into the Klops mixture, then moisten and soften it with a little of the hot vegetable stock.
4 Place spoonfuls of this mixture on the middle of each cabbage leaf and fold them up carefully, closing the sides underneath the final fold, to prevent the filling from coming out.
5 Sauté the onions, together with leftover smaller cabbage leaves, and put this in the bottom of a greased ovenproof dish.
6 Preheat the oven to 300°F/150°C/gas mark 2.
7 Arrange the cabbage rolls on top of the mixture.
8 Arrange the tomatoes and prunes on top of the rolls and season to taste with sea salt and freshly ground black pepper.
9 Mix the lemon juice and honey with the remaining vegetable stock and pour it over the rolls (make sure that the rolls are not completely covered with stock).
10 Cover the dish with its lid and bake in the preheated oven for about 3 hours, checking it periodically, adding more

stock as required and basting the rolls. Brown them with the lid off for the last 20 minutes of cooking, adding more honey or lemon juice if required. Serve with brown rice and salads.

Savoury Lentil and Vegetable Strudel

Imperial (Metric)		American
	Pastry	
½ lb (225g)	self-raising brown/wholewheat flour	2 cups
2 tsp	baking powder	2 tsp
	sea salt, freshly ground black pepper, onion salt and garlic salt	
1	free-range egg, beaten	1
2 fl oz (60ml)	sunflower oil	¼ cup
3-4 tbsp	water	3-4 tbsp
	sesame seeds, for sprinkling	
	Filling	
2	onions, chopped	2
2	carrots, chopped	2
3	medium potatoes, peeled and chopped	3
6 oz (170g)	peas	1 cup
1	tomato, chopped	1
1 tbsp	chopped fresh parsley	1 tbsp
½ lb (225g)	raw green lentils, cooked (3 cups when cooked)	1 cup
3 tbsp	tomato purée/paste	3 tbsp
2 tbsp	lemon juice	2 tbsp
2 heaped tsp	yeast extract *or* 1 tbsp soy sauce	2 heaped tsp
	sea salt, freshly ground black pepper and paprika	
	sunflower oil, for frying	

1 First make the pastry. Combine the flour, baking powder and seasonings to taste in a bowl and make a well in the centre.

2 Pour the egg and oil into the well and mix them into the flour to form a dough. Add the water a little at a time.
3 Knead the dough for a few minutes, then chill it until you are ready.
4 Now make the filling. Fry the onions until they are golden brown.
5 Steam or boil the carrots, potatoes and peas until they are just tender, then drain and add them to the pan with the onions. Stir them well and fry them lightly.
6 Add the tomatoes and parsley, mixing them in well.
7 Transfer the mixture to a large bowl and add the lentils, tomato purée, lemon juice, yeast extract or soy sauce and season to taste with sea salt, freshly ground black pepper and paprika. Mix everything together very well, taste it and adjust the seasoning if necessary. Add 2-3 tablespoons hot water and mix it in.
8 Preheat the oven to 375°F/190°C/gas mark 5.
9 Take the pastry out of the refrigerator and divide it into 2. Roll out each half into a rectangular shape to about an ⅛ inch (3mm) thickness. It is easier if you roll the pastry out on a sheet of lightly floured silicone paper.
10 Divide the filling equally between the two rectangles, placing it evenly down the middles. Allow ample margins all round the filling.
11 Fold the sides of the pastry over the filling and seal it in the middle by pressing it down gently with damp fingers and seal the ends, too.
12 Lift the silicone paper with the strudels, carefully to 1 or 2 baking sheets. Dampen them slightly and sprinkle the sesame seeds over the strudels.
13 Bake the strudels in the preheated oven for about 30 minutes, until they are golden brown, then serve them hot.

Note
If one strudel is sufficient for the number of people you are feeding, you can freeze one for another time.

Stuffed Aubergines

Imperial (Metric)		American
4 medium	aubergines/eggplants	4 medium
	sea salt and freshly ground black pepper	
2 medium	onions, finely chopped	2 medium
2	cloves garlic, crushed/minced	2
3 tbsp	corn oil	3 tbsp
1 tsp	paprika	1 tsp
2 tbsp	chopped fresh parsley	2 tbsp
3	soft, ripe tomatoes, skinned and chopped	3
3 oz (85g)	raw brown rice	½ cup
½ lb (225g)	tinned/canned chick peas/garbanzo beans, drained	1 cup
1 tbsp	polyunsaturated margarine	1 tbsp
⅓ pt (200ml)	hot water *or* vegetable stock	¾ cup
	fresh brown breadcrumbs	

1 Slice the aubergines (eggplants) in half lengthwise and sprinkle the cut surfaces with salt. Leave them for 30 minutes, then rinse them well under running water and pat dry.
2 Scoop out the pulp, leaving a little next to the skin so they keep their shape.
3 Sauté the onions and garlic in the oil until they are soft.
4 Season to taste with sea salt and freshly ground black pepper, then add the paprika, aubergine (eggplant) pulp, parsley and tomatoes. Cook until everything is soft.
5 At the same time, cook the rice in boiling water until it is tender then drain.
6 Preheat the oven to 350°F/180°C/gas mark 4.
7 Mix the aubergine (eggplant) mixture well with the rice and chick peas (garbanzos).
8 Spoon the mixture into the aubergine (eggplant) skins and sprinkle the breadcrumbs over the top.
9 Place them close together in an oiled ovenproof dish and dot the tops with margarine. Pour hot water or vegetable stock into the bottom of the dish.
10 Bake the aubergines (eggplants) in the preheated oven for about 30-40 minutes.

Galuptzi
(Spicy Cabbage Rolls)

Imperial (Metric)		American
1 medium	cabbage	1 medium
2 oz (55g)	raw brown rice	⅓ cup
1 × Klops recipe	(see pages 58-60),	1 × Klops recipe
	moistened with a little hot vegetable stock	
1 tbsp	chopped fresh parsley	1 tbsp
1 tsp	dried mixed herbs	1 tsp
1	clove garlic, crushed	1
1 tsp	yeast extract *or* soy sauce	1 tsp
	sea salt and freshly ground black pepper	
pinch	paprika	pinch
pinch	ginger	pinch
pinch	cinnamon	pinch
2	ripe tomatoes, skinned and chopped	2
1	onion, finely chopped	1
¾ pt (425ml)	vegetable stock, hot	2 cups
2-3 tsp	wholemeal/whole wheat flour	2-3 tsp

1 Put the cabbage in a pan of boiling water, salted water for about 5 minutes, just long enough to soften the leaves. When the cabbage is cool enough to handle, separate the leaves and wash them carefully under running, cold water.
2 Cook the rice in boiling water until it is tender, then drain it.
3 Mix the rice into the Klops mixture, then stir in the herbs, garlic, yeast extract or soy sauce, seasonings and spices.
4 Preheat the oven to 300°F/150°C/gas mark 2.
5 Place a spoonful of this mixture in the centre of each cabbage leaf and roll up carefully, closing the sides in first.
6 Place the remaining cabbage leaves in a well-greased ovenproof dish and put the cabbage rolls on top. Put the tomatoes, onion and hot stock over the top of them, cover the dish with its lid and bake in the preheated oven for about 3 hours. Baste it periodically, adding more stock if necessary. Remove the lid to let the rolls brown during the last 20 minutes of cooking. Thicken the gravy with the flour.
7 Drain the stock into a saucepan, holding the cabbage rolls

down with a spatula to stop them falling out, then thicken it into a gravy with the arrowroot or flour, cooking it over a fairly high heat, stirring, until it has thickened. Serve each person the cabbage rolls, cabbage, tomato and onion mixture and gravy.

Aubergine Quiche

Imperial (Metric)		American
	Pastry	
2 oz (55g)	polyunsaturated margarine	¼ cup
4 oz (115g)	self-raising brown/wholewheat flour	1 cup
pinch	sea salt	pinch
¼ tsp	dried mixed herbs	¼ tsp
2 fl oz (60ml), or less	milk *or* water	¼ cup, or less
	Filling	
1 medium	aubergine/eggplant	1 medium
1	onion, chopped	1
	sunflower oil, for frying	
14-oz (397-g)	tin/can tomatoes	14-oz
	sea salt and freshly ground black pepper	
2	free-range eggs, well beaten	2
¼ pt (140ml)	milk	⅔ cup
3 tbsp	grated/shredded Gouda cheese	3 tbsp
¼ tsp	paprika	¼ tsp

1 Make the pastry first by blending the margarine into the flour and seasonings until it looks like fine breadcrumbs.
2 Add sufficient milk or water to form a firm dough, then knead it lightly and chill for about 30 minutes.
3 Preheat the oven to 400°F/200°C/gas mark 6.
4 Roll the pastry out and line a greased ovenproof dish measuring about 8 by 10 inches (20 by 25cm).
5 Bake the pastry case (pie shell) blind (see page 17) in the preheated oven for about 10-15 minutes (leave the oven on).
6 Now make the filling. Peel and slice the aubergine

(eggplant), layer the slices in a colander or large plate, salting each layer, leave them for 30 minutes or until the bitter juices have been drawn out, then rinse them and pat them dry. Cut the slices into quarters.

7 Fry the onions and aubergine (eggplant) in a little oil until they are golden brown and have cooked through.

8 Drain the juice from the tomatoes (reserve it for another recipe), slice them and add them to the onion, aubergine (eggplant). Season to taste with sea salt and freshly ground black pepper and cook for about 5 minutes. Leave it to cool slightly.

9 Lightly dust the pastry case (pie shell) with flour, then pour in the aubergine (eggplant) mixture.

10 Add the milk to the eggs, beating them together well. Pour the mixture over the vegetables. Sprinkle the cheese and paprika over the top.

11 Bake in the oven for about 20 minutes until the quiche is firm and lightly golden brown. Serve it either hot or cold.

Note
Make double the quantity of pastry and freeze half of it to use next time.

Stuffed Courgettes

Imperial (Metric)		American
4	courgettes (zucchini), washed	4
4 oz (115g)	split red lentils	½ cup
8 fl oz (240ml)	vegetable stock, hot	1 cup
1	onion, finely chopped	1
	sunflower oil, for frying	
	sea salt and freshly ground black pepper	
1 tsp	ground cinnamon	1 tsp
2 tbsp	lemon juice	2 tbsp
2 tbsp	raisins (optional)	2 tbsp
4 tbsp	fresh wholemeal/whole wheat breadcrumbs	4 tbsp
2 tbsp	chopped English walnuts	2 tbsp

1 Put the courgettes (zucchini) in a pan of boiling water and boil them for about 5-10 minutes, then drain them.
2 Put the red lentils into the hot vegetable stock and bring it to the boil. Skim off the foam and then simmer them until all the liquid has been absorbed and the lentils are cooked and soft (add a little more hot water if the lentils are insufficiently cooked and cook them until they are).
3 Cut the courgettes (zucchini) in half lengthwise, scoop out the pulp and mash it.
4 Preheat the oven to 350°F/180°C/gas mark 4.
5 Fry the onions in a little oil until they are golden brown, then add them to the mashed courgette (zucchini) pulp, together with sea salt and freshly ground black pepper to taste, the cinnamon and lemon juice and stir in the lentils and raisins, if using.
6 Fill the courgette (zucchini) shells with the mixture and arrange them in an ovenproof casserole dish so that they support each other.
7 Sprinkle the breadcrumbs and walnuts over the filling.
8 Pour hot water and a squeeze of lemon juice into the casserole dish around the courgettes (zucchini), to reach halfway up the sides of them, then cover the casserole and bake in the preheated oven for 30-40 minutes until the filling is cooked. Serve the stuffed courgettes (zucchini) hot with brown rice.

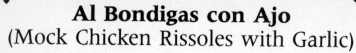

Al Bondigas con Ajo
(Mock Chicken Rissoles with Garlic)

Imperial (Metric)		American
2 medium	onions, finely chopped	2 medium
1	stick celery, finely chopped	1
1	clove garlic, crushed/minced	1
	sunflower oil, for frying	
1 lb (455g)	tofu	1 lb
3 tbsp	wholemeal/whole wheat flour	3 tbsp
3 tbsp	water	3 tbsp
1 tsp	sea salt	1 tsp
¼ tsp	freshly ground black pepper	¼ tsp
1 oz (30g)	fresh wholemeal breadcrumbs/ whole wheat bread crumbs	½ cup
2 tbsp	chopped fresh dill or parsley	2 tbsp
5	cloves garlic, sliced	5
2 tbsp	wholemeal/whole wheat flour	2 tbsp
⅔ pt (340ml)	hot water	1½ cups
3-4 tbsp	lemon juice	3-4 tbsp

1   Sauté the onion, celery and crushed (minced) garlic in a little oil until they have softened and are golden brown.
2   Drain the tofu, squeezing out as much liquid as possible (use a clean cloth to hold the tofu and twist it to squeeze out the liquid). Mash the tofu in a large bowl.
3   Mix the 3 tablespoons flour, water and seasonings to form a paste. Mix this into the tofu and then knead it for about 3-4 minutes. Drain the onion and celery mixture and stir it well into the tofu. Add the breadcrumbs and 1 tablespoon of the dill or parsley.
4   Form the mixture into rissole shapes and place them in a greased casserole dish.
5   Preheat the oven to 350°F/180°C/gas mark 4.
6   Lightly fry the sliced garlic in a little oil until they are golden brown, then stir in the 2 tablespoons of flour. Add the hot water gradually, stirring well continuously. Bring it to the boil, then let it cool slightly.

7 Pour this sauce evenly over the rissoles, then pour the lemon juice over the top.
8 Bake, covered in the preheated oven for 30-40 minutes.
9 Sprinkle the remaining dill or parsley over the top, then serve hot with brown rice.

Tomates Reyanados
(Baked Stuffed Tomatoes)

Imperial (Metric)		American
4 oz (115g)	lentils	½ cup
1	onion, finely chopped	1
1	clove garlic, crushed/minced	1
2 tbsp	sunflower oil	2 tbsp
1 tbsp	tomato purée/paste	1 tbsp
1 tsp	yeast extract *or* soy/soya sauce	1 tsp
2 tbsp	chopped fresh parsley	2 tbsp
2 tbsp	soft wholemeal breadcrumbs/ whole wheat bread crumbs	2 tbsp
2	free-range eggs	2
	sea salt and freshly ground black pepper	
4 large	firm tomatoes	4 large
2 tbsp	wholemeal/whole wheat flour, seasoned	2 tbsp
1 tsp	demerara sugar	1 tsp
1 tbsp	lemon juice	1 tbsp

1 Cook the lentils in plenty of water until they are soft. Drain, then mash them.
2 Lightly fry the onion and garlic in a little of the oil and add them to the lentils, together with the tomato purée and yeast extract or soy sauce and mix them together well.
3 Add half the parsley, breadcrumbs, one of the eggs, sea salt and freshly ground black pepper to taste and mix everything well together.
4 Cut each tomato in half and scoop out the pulp, reserving and mashing it.
5 Fill them with the lentil mixture. If there is any leftover

mixture, form it into little balls.

6 Preheat the oven to 350°F/180°C/gas mark 4.
7 Beat the remaining egg and dip the tomatoes, filled side down, into it, then into the seasoned flour. The little balls may also be dipped in the same way.
8 Fry the tomatoes for a few minutes cut side down, in a little oil. Fry the little balls too.
9 Arrange the tomatoes, filled side up, with the lentil balls, in a greased ovenproof casserole dish. Mix the reserved mashed tomato pulp with the sugar, lemon juice, remaining parsley and a little hot water or vegetable stock and pour it over the stuffed tomatoes and lentil balls.
10 Bake them, covered, in the preheated oven for about 30 minutes, uncovering them for the last 10-15 minutes of the cooking time. Serve them with brown rice and a green salad.

Spiced Tofu Casserole

Imperial (Metric)		American
1 medium	onion, chopped	1 medium
1	carrot, grated/shredded	1
1	stick celery, chopped	1
1	clove garlic, crushed/minced	1
	sunflower oil, for frying	
1 lb (455g)	tofu	1 lb
3 tbsp	wholemeal/whole wheat flour	3 tbsp
3 tbsp	water	3 tbsp
1 tsp	sea salt	1 tsp
¼ tsp	freshly ground black pepper	¼ tsp
1 tbsp	soy sauce	1 tbsp
½ cup	fresh wholemeal breadcrumbs/ whole wheat bread crumbs	½ cup
2 tbsp	chopped fresh parsley	2 tbsp
14-oz (397-g)	tin/can passata *or* tomato juice plus 2 tbsp tomato purée/paste	14-oz
2 tbsp	soy sauce	2 tbsp
	Garnish	
1 tbsp	finely chopped fresh parsley	1 tbsp

1 Sauté the onion, carrot, celery and garlic in a little oil until they have softened.
2 Drain the tofu, squeezing out as much liquid as possible (use a clean cloth to hold tofu and twist it to squeeze out the liquid). Mash the tofu in a large bowl.
3 Mix the flour, water and seasonings into a paste, then mix it into the tofu. Knead the tofu for about 3-4 minutes, then add the 1 tablespoon soy sauce, drain the fried vegetables and add them, together with the breadcrumbs, mix them all together very well.
4 Preheat the oven to 350°F/180°C/gas mark 4.
5 Form the mixture into rissole shapes and put them into a greased casserole dish. Mix passata or tomato juice mixture with the 2 tablespoons soy sauce and pour it evenly over the rissoles.
6 Cover the casserole dish and bake in the preheated oven for about 30-40 minutes. Then sprinkle the parsley over the top and serve hot with brown rice.

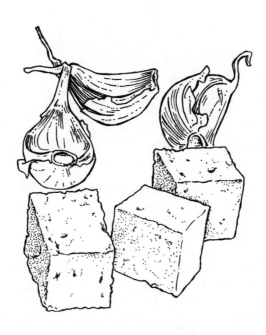

❖ Borekas with Mushroom Sauce ❖

Imperial (Metric)		American
	Pastry	
¾ lb (340g)	self-raising brown/wholewheat flour	3 cups
½ lb (225g)	soft white cheese	1 cup
7 oz (200g)	polyunsaturated margarine, cut up	1 cup less 2 tbsp
	pinch salt	
	Filling	
3-4 medium	potatoes, peeled	3-4 medium
4 oz (115g)	Gouda cheese, grated/shredded	1 cup
1 tsp	sea salt	1 tsp
½ tsp	freshly ground black pepper	½ tsp
1	free-range egg, beaten	1
2 tbsp	sesame seeds	2 tbsp
	Mushroom sauce	
1 medium	onion, chopped	1 medium
1	clove garlic, sliced	1
	sunflower oil, for frying	
½ lb (225g)	button mushrooms, chopped	2-3 cups
1 tbsp	chopped fresh parsley	1 tbsp
1 tbsp	wholemeal/whole wheat flour	1 tbsp
	sea salt, freshly ground black pepper and paprika	
¼ pt (140ml)	hot vegetable stock (or more)	⅔ cup

1 First make the pastry. Beat all the pastry ingredients together in a food processor to form a soft, smooth dough, adding a little more flour if necessary.
2 Chill the pastry for 3 hours.
3 When you are ready, make the filling. Boil and mash the potatoes. Combine them with the cheese, sea salt and freshly ground black pepper.
4 Preheat the oven to 425°F/220°C/gas mark 7.
5 Divide the pastry into 3 equal amounts, then roll each one out into a rectangle about 8 by 10 inches (20 by 25 cm)

to fit a pie or casserole dish of this size.

6 Lay the first pastry sheet in the greased pie dish and spread half the potato mixture over it. Lay the second pastry sheet over the mixture and spread the rest of the potato mixture over it. Lay the third pastry sheet over the mixture, seal and brush it with the beaten egg and sprinkle the sesame seeds over the top.

7 Bake in the preheated oven for 15-20 minutes.

8 Now make the mushroom sauce. Lightly fry the onion and garlic in a little oil until they have softened, then add the mushrooms, cook for about 10 minutes and add the parsley.

9 Stir in the flour, season to taste with sea salt, freshly ground black pepper and paprika. Slowly add the hot stock, stirring all the time, until it has thickened. Add hot water if sauce becomes too thick. Serve the sauce with the Borekas.

Cholent and Knaidel
(Bean and Barley Casserole with Dumplings)

Imperial (Metric)		American
	Cholent	
1 large	onion, finely chopped	1 large
	vegetable oil, for frying	
9 oz (260g)	butter/lima *or* mixed beans, boiled (see note)	1½ cups
½ lb (225g)	barley, well rinsed and boiled	1 cup
1	carrot, grated/shredded	1
2	tomatoes, chopped	2
2 tbsp	chopped fresh parsley	2 tbsp
1 tbsp	soy/soya sauce	1 tbsp
1 tbsp	tomato purée/paste	1 tbsp
2 tbsp	wholemeal/whole wheat flour	2 tbsp
1 tsp	paprika	1 tsp
	sea salt, freshly ground black pepper and garlic salt	
2 large	potatoes, peeled and thickly sliced	2 large
	hot vegetable stock, to cover	
	Knaidels (dumplings)	

95

6 oz (170g)	wholemeal/whole wheat flour	1½ cups
	sea salt and freshly ground black pepper	
3 oz (85g)	polyunsaturated margarine	⅓ cup
2 tbsp	grated/shredded onion, lightly sautéed in oil	2 tbsp
1	potato, finely grated/shredded	1
1 tsp	chopped fresh parsley	1 tsp
1	free-range egg (optional)	1
1 tsp	yeast extract *or* soy/soya sauce	1 tsp
2 fl oz (60ml)	cold water	4 tbsp

1 First make the Cholent. Fry the onion in a little of the oil until it is golden brown.

2 Put the onion, cooked beans, cooked barley, carrot, tomato and parsley in the bottom of an ovenproof casserole dish, which should have a tightly fitting lid. Add the soy sauce and tomato purée.

3 Preheat the oven to 350°F/180°C/gas mark 4.

4 Mix together the flour, paprika and seasonings and add them to the casserole, covering the beans, barley and vegetables and mix it in well.

5 Cover the vegetables with the potatoes and season to taste with sea salt and freshly ground black pepper.

6 Pour sufficient hot vegetable stock into the casserole to cover all the ingredients.

7 Cover with a lid and bake in the preheated oven for about 45 minutes.

8 Meanwhile make the Knaidels. Combine the flour, and seasonings and rub in the margarine until the mixture resembles fine breadcrumbs.

9 Add the sautéd onion, grated potato, parsley, egg (if using), yeast extract or soy sauce and enough of the cold water to make a soft doughy mixture.

10 Form the mixture into dumplings, about the size of walnuts.

11 Remove the casserole from the oven and place the dumplings on top of the vegetables.

12 Add more hot vegetable stock up to the level of the dumplings and replace the lid. Lower the oven to 225°F/110°C/gas mark ¼ or use a slow cooker/crockpot.

13 Leave in the oven/slow cooker/crockpot overnight until required.

Note

The beans should be checked, soaked overnight and boiled very well for at least 20-30 minutes or until they are cooked before being used in the casserole.

Mejedra
(Rice and Lentil Pilaff)

Imperial (Metric)		American
½ lb (225g)	brown rice, rinsed	1 cup
1 tsp	sea salt	1 tsp
1 tsp	dried mixed herbs	1 tsp
	hot vegetable stock, as required	
3	onions, thinly sliced	3
1 fl oz (30ml)	sunflower oil, or more if needed	2 tbsp
2 oz (55g)	blanched almonds, chopped	½ cup
2 tbsp	raisins	2½ tbsp
½ lb (225g)	brown lentils, soaked overnight	1 cup
	freshly ground black pepper	

1 Put the rice in a pan with the salt, half the herbs and 2½ times its volume of hot vegetable stock. Bring it to the boil, then simmer it gently until all the stock has been absorbed (about 30 minutes). Set aside.
2 Sauté two thirds of the onions in the oil until they are golden brown.
3 Add the nuts and fry gently for a few minutes.
4 Rinse the raisins under hot running water and add them to the onion and nut mixture. Set this mixture aside.
5 Gently fry the remaining onion in a little oil in a saucepan, add the lentils, the rest of the herbs and enough vegetable stock to cover.
6 Bring to the boil and simmer until the lentils are soft (about 1 hour), adding more water if necessary.
7 Combine the rice and lentils, add a little hot stock, sea salt and freshly ground black pepper to taste and bring to the boil again.
8 Simmer the mixture gently over a very low heat until all the liquid has been absorbed. Serve with the onion, almond and raisin mixture piled on top.

Bobotie
(Curried Casserole)

Imperial (Metric)		American
½ lb (225g)	Tvp soya mince (soya protein grits)	2 cups
1 slice	wholemeal/whole wheat bread	1 slice
⅓ pt (200ml)	milk *or* soya milk	¾ cup
1	onion, finely chopped	1
2 tbsp	corn oil	2 tbsp
2	tomatoes, skinned and chopped	2
1 tbsp	curry powder	1 tbsp
1 tbsp	tomato purée/paste	1 tbsp
1 tbsp	soy/soya sauce	1 tbsp
2 tsp	demerara sugar	2 tsp
2 tbsp	cider vinegar	2 tbsp
	sea salt and freshly ground black pepper	
1 tsp	mixed dried herbs	1 tsp
2	free-range eggs	2
1 oz (30g)	almonds, chopped	¼ cup

1 Rehydrate the Tvp soya mince as directed on the packaging.
2 Soak the bread in a little of the milk and then mash it well with a fork.
3 Sauté the onion in the oil until it is golden brown then add the tomatoes.
4 Preheat the oven to 350°F/180°C/gas mark 4.
5 Add the curry powder, tomato purée, soy sauce, sugar, vinegar, seasonings and herbs to the onion mixture, stir them into it well and cook for a few minutes.
6 Combine this mixture with the rehydrated Tvp mince, the mashed bread and one of the eggs, beaten.
7 Spoon it into a greased casserole dish and bake in the preheated oven for about 30 minutes. Leave the oven on.
8 Beat the second egg very well with the remaining milk, season to taste with a little sea salt and freshly ground black pepper and pour it over the Tvp soya mince mixture.
9 Sprinkle the almonds over the top and return the casserole to the oven for about 20-30 minutes. Serve it hot with brown rice and salads.

Variation
Substitute cooked, mashed lentils for the Tvp soya mince/grits.

 ——————————————————————

Soya Bean Goulash

Imperial (Metric)		American
1	onion, chopped	1
1	green pepper, deseeded and chopped	1
3 tbsp	corn oil	3 tbsp
1 tbsp	paprika	1 tbsp
1 tbsp	caraway seeds	1 tbsp
	garlic salt	
1	ripe tomato, skinned and chopped	1
2 tbsp	tomato purée/paste	2 tbsp
1 tsp	yeast extract *or* soy/soya sauce	1 tsp
1 tbsp	chopped fresh parsley	1 tbsp
4 oz (115g)	mushrooms, chopped	2 cups
½ lb (225g)	cooked soya beans	1 cup
	sea salt and freshly ground black pepper	
¾ pt (425ml)	hot vegetable stock	2 cups
3-4	parboiled potatoes, chopped	3-4

1 Sauté the onion and green pepper in the oil until they have softened.
2 Stir in the paprika, caraway seeds and garlic salt to taste, and sauté for another 5 minutes.
3 Preheat the oven to 300°F/150°C/gas mark 2.
4 Add the tomato, tomato purée, yeast extract or soy sauce, parsley and mushrooms and cook for about 10 more minutes.
5 Transfer the mixture to an ovenproof casserole that has a lid.
6 Add the cooked beans, season to taste with sea salt and freshly ground black pepper and the hot stock.
7 Bake in the preheated oven for 2-2½ hours.
8 About 1 hour before serving, add the potatoes. When it is cooked, serve it straight away with brown rice and salad.

Note

Dry soya beans may be placed in water and kept in the refrigerator for 3 days, changing the water and rinsing the beans well every day. They may then be brought to the boil, rinsed well and cooked for 2-3 hours until they are ready for use. Those not wanted immediately may be frozen and kept for another time.

Tinned (canned) soya beans may be used for this recipe if you do not have the time or inclination to cook them yourself.

❖ 4 ❖
Side Dishes

❖ ──────────────────────────────────── ❖

Fritada de Espinaca
(Spinach Soufflé)

Imperial (Metric)		American
1 lb (450g)	frozen, cooked spinach, thawed/defrosted, plus liquid	1 lb
4 oz (115g)	cheese, grated/shredded	1 cup
3	free-range eggs, well beaten	3
1 oz (30g)	soft wholemeal/whole wheat bread crumbs	½ cup
¼ pt (140ml)	milk	⅔ cup
	sea salt and freshly ground black pepper	
pinch	nutmeg	pinch

1 Preheat the oven to 350°F/180°C/gas mark 4.
2 Combine all the ingredients mixing them together well.
3 Pour the mixture into a well-greased casserole dish.
4 Bake in the preheated oven for about 30 minutes or until the soufflé has set and is cooked.

Moroccan Olives

Imperial (Metric)		American
1 lb (445g)	tin/can stoned/pitted green olives	4 cups
1 medium	onion, finely chopped	1 medium
1 small	clove garlic, crushed/minced	1 small
	vegetable oil, for frying	
4	fresh, ripe tomatoes	4
3 oz (85g)	tomato purée/paste	⅓ cup
	paprika and freshly ground black pepper	
	hot water, as necessary	
	sea salt	

1　Put the olives in a pan of water, bring it to the boil, drain, fill the pan with fresh water and repeat the process until they have been boiled and drained 3 times.
2　Fry the onion and garlic in a little oil until the onion is translucent.
3　Skin and mash the tomatoes well, then add them to the onion mixture and fry them until they are well cooked.
4　Add the tomato purée, season to taste with paprika and freshly ground black pepper and add the water.
5　Cook the mixture over a low heat, adding 1-1½ cups hot water slowly at intervals.
6　Mix in the olives, adding sea salt to taste.
7　Serve them hot with roast or jacket potatoes and a main course of your choice such as Seniyeh or Savoury Lentil and Vegetable Strudel (see pages 62 and 83) or other main course of your choice, or let them cool, chill them and serve them cold as a salad.

Onions with Fruit

Imperial (Metric)		American
1 tbsp	tomato purée/paste	1 tbsp
2 tbsp	sunflower oil	2 tbsp
	juice of 1 lemon	
2 tsp	honey	2 tsp
¼ pt (140ml)	water	⅔ cup
	sea salt and freshly ground black pepper	
1 lb (455g)	small onions	1 lb
4	dried pears *or* 1 fresh pear	4
6	dried prunes	6
6	dried apricots	6

1 Preheat the oven to 325°F/170°C/gas mark 3.
2 Mix the tomato purée, oil, lemon juice, honey and water together and bring the mixture to the boil. Add a pinch of sea salt and freshly ground black pepper.
3 Add the onions, cover the saucepan and simmer for about 10 minutes.
4 If using a fresh pear, peel and slice it into 8 segments.
5 Put the pears or pear segments into an ovenproof dish, add the prunes and apricots and stir in the simmered onions and the liquid, adding more water if necessary to cover the fruit.
6 Bake in the preheated oven for about 40 minutes or until all the ingredients are tender.
7 This is a delicious accompaniment to Klops (see pages 58-60) or Koklaten (see pages 64-6).

Orez Parsi
(Persian Rice)

Imperial (Metric)		American
2 oz (55g)	raisins	⅓ cup
2 oz (55g)	currants *or* sultanas/ golden seedless raisins	⅓ cup
4 oz (115g)	prunes	⅔ cup
4 oz (115g)	soft, dried apricots	⅔ cup
2 oz (55g)	polyunsaturated margarine	¼ cup
2 oz (55g)	chopped almonds	½ cup
1⅓ pt (743ml)	water	3 cups
½ lb (225g)	brown rice	1 cup
	sea salt and freshly ground black pepper	
¼ tsp	ground cinnamon	¼ tsp

1 Pour boiling water over the dried fruit, cover and leave them to soak for 30-40 minutes.
2 Drain the fruit and chop the prunes and apricots into small pieces.
3 Heat the margarine in a saucepan and gently sauté the raisins, currants or sultanas (golden seedless raisins), prunes, apricots and chopped almonds for 5-10 minutes.
4 Pour the water over the fruit and nut mixture, add the rice, sea salt and freshly ground black pepper to taste and the cinnamon, stirring everything together.
5 Bring to the boil, reduce the heat, cover and simmer over a low heat until the rice is cooked, then serve it hot.

Tzimmes

Imperial (Metric)		American
2 medium	onions, finely chopped	2 medium
2	cloves garlic, crushed/minced	2
2 tbsp	sunflower oil	2 tbsp
1 lb (455g)	carrots, grated/shredded	1 lb
2 tbsp	ground almonds	2 tbsp
1	free-range egg	1
¼ tsp	freshly ground black pepper	¼ tsp
1 tsp	lemon juice	1 tsp
2-3 oz (55-85g)	fresh wholemeal/whole wheat bread crumbs	1-1½ cups

1 Preheat the oven to 400°F/200°C/gas mark 6.
2 Sauté the onions and garlic in the oil until they have softened and are golden brown.
3 Add the carrots and cook them for 5 minutes, then remove the pan from the heat.
4 Combine this mixture with the rest of the ingredients, adding just enough breadcrumbs to make a firm consistency.
5 Spoon the mixture into a greased ovenproof casserole dish and bake in the preheated oven for about 30 minutes.

Courgettes and Tomatoes

Imperial (Metric)		American
1 large	onion, chopped	1 large
2	cloves garlic, crushed/minced	2
2 tbsp	chopped green pepper	2 tbsp
2 tbsp	corn oil	2 tbsp
	sea salt and freshly ground black pepper	
1 tbsp	chopped fresh parsley	1 tbsp
¼ tsp	dried oregano	¼ tsp
3 large	ripe tomatoes, skinned and chopped	3 large
4-5	courgettes/zucchini, sliced, unpeeled	4-5

1 Sauté the onion, garlic and green pepper in the oil until they have softened.
2 Season to taste with sea salt and freshly ground black pepper, parsley and oregano. Add tomatoes and cook it over a low heat for about 5 minutes.
3 To this mixture, add the courgettes (zucchini) and cook gently until they have softened (about 20 minutes).

Mushrooms in Wine Sauce

Imperial (Metric)		American
1 medium	onion, finely chopped	1 medium
2	cloves garlic	2
	vegetable oil, for frying	
¾ lb (340g)	button mushrooms, washed and halved or quartered	¾ lb
1 tbsp	cider vinegar	1 tbsp
3 tbsp	wine (red *or* white)	3 tbsp
3 tbsp	tomato purée/paste	3 tbsp
1 tbsp	parsley, chopped	1 tbsp
	sea salt and freshly ground black pepper	

1 Preheat the oven to 350°F/180°C/gas mark 4.
2 Sauté the onions and garlic lightly in a little oil.
3 Put the mushrooms in an ovenproof casserole dish.
4 Combine the vinegar, wine, tomato purée and parsley and pour this over the mushrooms.
5 Pour the sautéed onion and garlic, together with the oil in which they were cooked, over the mushrooms and mix them in.
6 Season to taste with sea salt and freshly ground black pepper.
7 Cover the casserole dish tightly with a well-fitting lid or a layer of silicone paper topped with foil so the lid then fits tightly.
8 Bake in the preheated oven for about 20-30 minutes or until the mushrooms are tender.

Crumbed Cauliflower

Imperial (Metric)		American
1	cauliflower, washed in salted water	1
2 oz (55g)	dried wholemeal/whole wheat bread crumbs	½ cup
	sea salt and freshly ground black pepper	
½ tsp	dried mixed herbs	½ tsp
2 tbsp	coarsely chopped nuts	2 tbsp
2 oz (55g)	butter *or* polyunsaturated margarine	¼ cup

1 Preheat the oven to 375°F/190°C/gas mark 5.
2 Divide the cauliflower into florets and boil them in a little water or steam them until they are tender, then put them into a greased ovenproof casserole.
3 Mix the breadcrumbs, sea salt and freshly ground black pepper, herbs and nuts together and sprinkle this over the cauliflower florets.
4 Dab the cauliflower with the butter or margarine and brown it in the preheated oven for about 10-15 minutes.

Potato Kugel

Imperial (Metric)		American
4-6 medium	potatoes	4-6 medium
1 small	onion	1 small
2 tbsp	butter *or* polyunsaturated margarine	2 tbsp
2	free-range eggs, beaten	2
2 tbsp	wholemeal/whole wheat flour	2 tbsp
1 tsp	sea salt	1 tsp
1 tsp	baking powder	1 tsp

1 Preheat the oven to 350°F/180°C/gas mark 4.
2 Grate (shred) the potatoes and onion finely.
3 Melt the butter or margarine in an ovenproof casserole and mix in the potato and onion, coating them in the butter or margarine.
4 Add the remaining ingredients and mix them together well.
5 Bake in the preheated oven until the Kugel is golden brown and firm (about 1-1½ hours).

Aubergine Relish

Imperial (Metric)		American
1 large	aubergine/eggplant	1 large
1 large	red pepper, deseeded and chopped	1 large
1 medium	onion, chopped	1 medium
	sunflower *or* olive oil, for frying	
2	ripe tomatoes, skinned and chopped	2
2-3 tbsp	lemon juice	2-3 tbsp
1-2 tbsp	raw cane sugar	1-2 tbsp
	sea salt and freshly ground black pepper	

1 Prick the skin of the aubergine (eggplant) in a number of places.

108

2 Preheat the oven to 400°F/200°C/gas mark 6 and bake it for about 40-50 minutes or until it is tender.
3 Fry the pepper and onion until the onions have softened and are transparent.
4 Add the tomatoes.
5 Slice the aubergine (eggplant) and scoop out the pulp. Mash it well and add it to the pepper, onion and tomato mixture.
6 Add the lemon juice, sugar and season to taste with sea salt and freshly ground black pepper, and simmer gently for about 20 minutes.
7 Check the seasoning and adjust if necessary.
8 Let it cool and then chill for a day to allow the flavours to blend.
9 Serve it as a relish with main courses, for example with Lahne be Sahem or Mejedra (see pages 65 and 97).

Sweet and Sour Cabbage

Imperial (Metric)		**American**
1	onion, chopped	1
2 tbsp	sunflower oil	2 tbsp
1 lb (450g)	red cabbage, shredded	4 cups
1 large	apple, grated	1 large
2 fl oz (60ml)	vegetable stock	¼ cup
	sea salt and freshly ground black pepper	
juice of	½ lemon	juice of
2 tsp	honey	2 tsp
2 tbsp	sweet red wine (optional)	2 tbsp

1 Preheat the oven to 350°F/180°C/gas mark 4.
2 Sauté the onion in the oil for a few minutes.
3 Add the cabbage, apple, stock, season to taste with sea salt and freshly ground black pepper, the lemon juice and honey and cook gently for about 15 minutes.
4 Add the wine, if using, then spoon the mixture into an ovenproof casserole dish with a lid.
5 Bake in the preheated oven for about 1-1½ hours.

Gemüse Kugel
(Vegetable Kugel)

Imperial (Metric)		American
2	eating apples, peeled and cored	2
2 medium	carrots, scrubbed	2 medium
2 medium	potatoes, peeled	2 medium
2	courgettes/zucchini, washed	2
2-3 tbsp	raw cane sugar	2-3 tbsp
4 oz (115g)	wholemeal/whole wheat flour	1 cup
1 tsp	ground cinnamon	1 tsp
¼ tsp	ground ginger	¼ tsp
	sea salt and freshly ground black pepper	
2 fl oz (60ml)	sunflower oil	¼ cup
1-2 tbsp	sesame seeds	1-2 tbsp

1 Preheat the oven to 350°F/180°C/gas mark 4.
2 Grate (shred) all the fruit and vegetables finely, then mix in the sugar, flour, cinnamon, ginger and season to taste with sea salt and freshly ground black pepper.
3 Add the oil, stirring it in well. Spoon the mixture into a greased ovenproof casserole dish, sprinkle with sesame seeds, cover and bake in the preheated oven for 1 hour, then uncover the dish and bake for 10-20 more minutes until it is golden brown.

Fasoulia
(Sephardic Green Beans)

Imperial (Metric)		American
1 lb (450g)	fresh French *or* runner beans/ fresh fine *or* young green beans	1 lb
1 small	onion, finely chopped	1 small
1	clove garlic, crushed/minced	1
2 tbsp	sunflower oil	2 tbsp
2-3 large	ripe tomatoes, skinned and chopped	2-3 large
4 fl oz (120ml)	hot water	½ cup
	sea salt and freshly ground black pepper	

1 Preheat the oven to 350°F/180°C/gas mark 4.
2 Wash, top and tail the beans, then cut them into slices.
3 Lightly fry the onion and garlic in the oil for a few minutes, then add the beans, tomatoes, water and season to taste with sea salt and freshly ground black pepper.
4 Bake, covered, in the preheated oven or simmer on top of the cooker for 20-30 minutes or until the beans are tender.

Carrot and Potato Tzimmes

Imperial (Metric)		American
1 lb (450g)	fresh carrots	1 lb
1	parsnip *or* sweet potato/yam	1
2 large	potatoes	2 large
1 small	onion, quartered	1 small
2 oz (55g)	cabbage, shredded	½ cup
2 tbsp	sunflower seed oil	2 tbsp
7 fl oz (200ml)	hot vegetable stock	¾ cup
2 tsp	wholemeal/whole wheat flour	2 tsp
1 tbsp	demerara sugar	1 tbsp
	sea salt and freshly ground black pepper	
8-10	prunes, soaked and cut into halves (plus liquid)	8-10

1 Clean and trim the root vegetables and cut them into small pieces.
2 Lightly fry the onion and cabbage in the oil until the onions have softened and transfer the mixture to an ovenproof casserole with a lid.
3 Cook the root vegetables in the stock over a low heat for about 20-30 minutes, then transfer them to the casserole dish using a slotted spoon and reserve the stock.
4 Towards the end of the vegetables' cooking time, turn the oven on to 350°F/180°C/gas mark 4.
5 Mix the flour, sugar, salt and pepper with a little cold water to form a creamy liquid. Slowly add the reserved stock, stirring and pour this over the vegetables in the casserole dish.
6 Place the prune halves among the vegetables and add the prune liquid.
7 Cover and bake in the preheated oven for about 30-40 minutes, until all the vegetables are tender. Add more water or stock if necessary.
8 Uncover and bake until the top browns slightly.

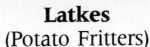

Latkes
(Potato Fritters)

Makes 12-15 fritters

Imperial (Metric)		American
1 lb (450g)	potatoes, peeled	1 lb
1 medium	onion, peeled	1 medium
2	free-range eggs	2
1 tsp	sea salt	1 tsp
	freshly ground black pepper	
1 oz (30g)	wholemeal/whole wheat flour	¼ cup
1 tsp	baking powder	1 tsp
	vegetable oil, for frying	

1 Grate (shred) the potatoes and onion, but not too coarsely. Strain off the liquid.
2 Beat the eggs until they are frothy and add them to the potato and onion mixture, together with the sea salt and freshly ground black pepper to taste.
3 Stir the flour and baking powder together and mix them into the potato mixture.
4 Heat a little oil in a frying pan (skillet) and drop tablespoons of the mixture into the hot oil in batches.
5 Fry the Latkes on both sides until they are golden brown.
6 Keep them warm in the oven and serve them warm. They are often served with apple sauce.

❖ 5 ❖
Salads

❖ ──────────────────────────────────── ❖

Garden Salad

Imperial (Metric)		American
3	firm, ripe tomatoes	3
1 medium	green pepper	1 medium
½-1	cucumber	½-1
1	stick/stalk celery, chopped	1
1	carrot, cut into strips	1
6-8	radishes	6-8
2	spring onions/scallions, chopped	2
	lettuce leaves	
2 tbsp	chopped fresh parsley	2 tbsp

1 Wash the tomatoes and cut them into small, bite-sized pieces.
2 Wash the green pepper, remove the seeds and chop it finely.
3 Wash, but do not peel, the cucumber and cut it into bite-sized pieces.
4 Arrange all the vegetables attractively on a large serving plate (platter) lined with lettuce leaves.
5 Chill and serve it with the salad dressing of your choice, sprinkling the parsley over the top.

Cholemady
(Pickled Vegetables)

Imperial (Metric)		American
1⅓ pt (680ml)	water	3 cups
⅔ pt (340ml)	white malt vinegar	1½ cups
2 tbsp	raw cane sugar	2 tbsp
2 tsp	sea salt	2 tsp
5	bay leaves	5
10	peppercorns	10
½ small	white cabbage, thinly sliced, core removed	½ small
¼ small	cauliflower, divided into florets, cut into bite-sized pieces	¼ small
2	carrots, sliced	2
1	cucumber, sliced	1
½	red pepper, deseeded and sliced	½
½	green pepper, deseeded and sliced	½
2	cloves garlic, chopped	2
1	onion, finely sliced	1

1 Boil the water, vinegar, sugar, sea salt, bay leaves and peppercorns in large saucepan.
2 Add the vegetables and boil for about 5 minutes.
3 Let them cool then transfer the vegetables, with the cooking liquid, into sterilized pickling jars with lids. Chill them for 2 days before using and keep them chilled after opening. Use them as a salad.

Note:
Remove the bay leaves before serving. **Do not eat bay leaves** as they are very sharp.

Lentil Salad

Imperial (Metric)		American
10 oz (280g)	brown lentils	1½ cups
	Salad Dressing (see page 127), made with	
	olive oil *or* sunflower oil and lemon juice	
	sea salt and freshly ground black pepper	
1 small	spring onion/scallion, finely chopped	1 small
2 tbsp	chopped fresh parsley	2 tbsp
	Garnish	
1	tomato, cut into segments	1
4-6	olives	4-6

1 Rinse the lentils well under running cold water and soak them overnight in cold water in the refrigerator. Rinse them again under cold running water.
2 Put the drained lentils in a saucepan, cover them with cold water, bring to the boil and simmer gently for about 1 hour until the lentils are tender. Drain them (reserve any remaining liquid for use as stock in other dishes).
3 Liberally sprinkle the hot lentils with the Salad Dressing and season to taste with sea salt and freshly ground black pepper.
4 Serve cold, mixing in the chopped spring onion (scallion) and more Salad Dressing just before serving.
5 Sprinkle with the parsley and decorate with the tomato segments and olives.

Avocado and Papaya Salad

Imperial (Metric)		American
1 large	ripe avocado	1 large
3 tbsp	lemon juice, plus extra for sprinkling over the fruits	3 tbsp
1	ripe papaya	1
1	sweet, seedless orange	1
	lettuce leaves	
2-3 tbsp	strawberries, blackberries, raspberries	2-3 tbsp
1 tbsp	sunflower oil	1 tbsp
1-2 tsp	light demerara sugar	1-2 tsp
	sea salt and freshly ground black pepper	

Garnish

small bunch	watercress, washed and dried	small bunch

1 Peel and dice the avocado and sprinkle lemon juice over it immediately to prevent it discolouring.
2 Peel the papaya, remove the seeds, dice the flesh and sprinkle lemon juice over it.
3 Peel the orange and cut it into thin, horizontal slices.
4 Place the orange slices on a bed of lettuce leaves. Arrange the avocado and papaya pieces on the orange slices, mixing them evenly.
5 Mix the sunflower oil, the 3 tablespoons lemon juice, the sugar and sea salt and freshly ground black pepper very well and pour it over the salad.
6 Scatter the berries over the fruit.
7 Garnish with watercress leaves.

Spinach Salad

Imperial (Metric)		American
1 lb (450g)	fresh spinach leaves	1 lb
2 oz (55g)	mushrooms, sliced	1 cup
2 small	spring onions/scallions, finely chopped	2 small
1	free-range egg, hard-boiled/hard-cooked and mashed	1
	garlic-flavoured wholemeal/whole wheat croûtons (optional)	

1 Wash the spinach leaves very well under cold running water and inspect them carefully to make sure they are clean and free of insects, then pat them dry. Tear them into small pieces and put them into a salad bowl.
2 Scatter the mushrooms, onion (scallion), egg and croûtons, if using, over the spinach leaves. Serve with Salad Dressing (see page 127).

Note
To make the croûtons, cut 2 slices of bread into small pieces (the size of a pea) and fry lightly in vegetable oil until golden. Add sliced garlic and ¼ teaspoonful mixed herbs to the frying oil.

Pickled Cucumber Salad

Imperial (Metric)		American
2 large	cucumbers *or* 4-5 small cucumbers, washed	2 large
2	cloves garlic, sliced	2
⅔ pt (340ml)	cider vinegar	1½ cups
4 fl oz (120ml)	cold water	½ cup
2 tbsp	demerara sugar	2 tbsp
1 tsp	sea salt	1 tsp
	freshly ground black pepper	
1 tsp	dill seed (optional)	1 tsp

1　Slice the cucumbers.
2　Boil together the garlic, vinegar, water, sugar, sea salt and freshly ground black pepper.
3　Add the cucumber and boil the slices for just a few minutes, then remove them from the heat.
4　Leave them to cool then transfer them and the cooking liquid to a sterilized jar, adding the dill seed, if using, then refrigerate until needed.

Cabbage and Carrot Salad

Imperial (Metric)		American
6 oz (170g)	carrots, grated/shredded	1 cup
½ lb (225g)	cabbage, shredded	2 cups
1	spring onion/scallion, finely chopped	1
a few	lettuce leaves, shredded	a few
2 tbsp	chopped almonds	2 tbsp
2 tbsp	raisins	2 tbsp
2½ tbsp	sunflower oil	2½ tbsp
juice of	½ lemon	juice of
	celery salt	
	sea salt and freshly ground black pepper	
	Garnish	
½	orange, sliced	½

1　Combine the carrots, cabbage, spring onion (scallion), lettuce leaves, almonds and raisins, mixing them together well.
2　Mix the oil and lemon juice with a little water and celery salt, sea salt and freshly ground black pepper and pour this over the salad.
3　Decorate with the slices of orange and serve the salad cold.

❖ ———————————————————————————— ❖

Cabbage and Apple Salad

Imperial (Metric)		American
½	white cabbage	½
½	red cabbage	½
1 tsp	sea salt	1 tsp
2	Granny Smith apples	2
1 tsp	caraway seeds	1 tsp
2 tbsp	sunflower oil	2 tbsp
⅓ pt (200ml)	cider vinegar	¾ cup
1 tbsp	raw cane sugar	1 tbsp

1 Wash and grate (shred) the green and red cabbage. Add the salt.
2 Mix the two colours of cabbage together until they are well distributed, using your hands.
3 Peel and grate (shred) the apples and mix them into the cabbage.
4 Mix in the caraway seeds and the oil.
5 Boil together the vinegar, sugar and a pinch of salt.
6 Pour this dressing over the salad.
7 Chill it until it is needed.

❖ ———————————————————————————— ❖

Apple Salad

Imperial (Metric)		American
4	juicy, red eating apples, washed	4
½	lemon	½
	apple *or* orange juice as required	
2 oz (55g)	grapes, washed	2 oz
1 large	sweet orange	1 large
1	stick/stalk celery, washed	1
2 tbsp	chopped walnuts/English walnuts	2 tbsp
1 tbsp	pumpkin seeds	1 tbsp
¼ pt (140ml)	natural/unsweetened yogurt	⅔ cup
1 tsp	honey	1 tsp

1 Cut the apples, unpeeled, into small pieces and put them in a bowl. Squeeze the lemon and pour a little apple or orange juice over them to stop them discolouring.
2 Halve the grapes and remove the pips (seeds).
3 Peel the orange and cut the segments into small pieces.
4 Chop the celery finely.
5 Mix the apple, grapes, orange and celery together, chill, then, when you are ready to serve, sprinkle the walnuts and pumpkin seeds over the top.
6 Mix the honey into the yogurt and mix this dressing well into the salad. Alternatively, dress your salad with a plain salad dressing if preferred.

Celery Salad

Imperial (Metric)		American
2	sticks celery, washed	2
3 medium	tomatoes	3 medium
¼	cucumber	¼
10	olives, stoned/pitted	10
2 tbsp	finely chopped fresh parsley	2 tbsp
2 tbsp	finely chopped fresh chives	2 tbsp
1 tbsp	lemon juice	1 tbsp
3 tbsp	olive *or* sunflower oil	3 tbsp
	sea salt and freshly ground black pepper	

1 Chop the celery into fine pieces, then chop the tomatoes and cucumber and slice the olives.
2 Combine all the vegetables together in a bowl with the herbs.
3 Mix the lemon juice and oil together well, season to taste with sea salt and freshly ground black pepper and pour this dressing over the salad.

Crunchy Lettuce Salad

Imperial (Metric)   American

about 8-10	mixed lettuce leaves	about 8-10
4-6 slices	fresh *or* tinned/canned pineapple, chopped	4-6 slices
1	stick celery/celery stalk, chopped	1
1 tbsp	chopped walnuts/English walnuts	1 tbsp
1 tbsp	sunflower seeds (lightly toasted)	1 tbsp
1 tbsp	pumpkin seeds	1 tbsp

1 Wash the lettuce well and pat dry or use a lettuce spinner so it is not damp.
2 Tear the lettuce into small pieces and put them into a bowl. Add the pineapple and celery.
3 Just before serving, sprinkle the nuts and seeds over the top.

Potato Salad

Imperial (Metric)   American

4-6	medium potatoes, scrubbed	4-6
2	spring onions/scallions, chopped	2
¼	red pepper, deseeded	¼
2 tbsp	pickled *or* fresh cucumber, chopped	2 tbsp
3 tbsp	chopped fresh parsley	3 tbsp
4 tbsp	mayonnaise	4 tbsp
1 tbsp	lemon juice	1 tbsp
2 tbsp	sunflower oil	2 tbsp
	sea salt and freshly ground black pepper	
	Garnish	
1	free-range egg, hard-boiled/hard-cooked and mashed (optional)	1

1 Steam or boil the potatoes until they are tender. When they are cool enough to handle, peel and dice them and put them

into a bowl. Mix in the spring onion (scallion), red pepper, cucumber and parsley, reserving a pinch or so for garnishing.

3 Mix the mayonnaise well with the lemon juice and oil and season to taste with sea salt and freshly ground black pepper. Then pour the dressing over the potatoes, stirring it in gently so as not to break up the potato.

4 Garnish with the egg, if using, and the reserved parsley.

❖ ———————————————————————— ❖
Raw Beetroot and Carrot Salad

Imperial (Metric)		American
2 medium	beetroots/beets, uncooked	2 medium
2	carrots	2
1	eating apple	1
2 tbsp	olive oil	2 tbsp
1 tbsp	lemon juice	1 tbsp
	sea salt and freshly ground black pepper	
2 tbsp	chopped fresh parsley	2 tbsp

1 Peel and grate the beetroots (beets), carrots and apples.
2 Mix the olive oil and lemon juice together, season to taste with sea salt and freshly ground black pepper and pour the dressing over the salad. Add more oil and lemon juice if it looks a little too dry.
3 Sprinkle the parsley over the top and serve with Koklaten (see pages 64-6), nut roasts or as desired.

Tabbouleh

Imperial (Metric)		American
4 oz	bulgar wheat	⅔ cup
½ pt (285ml)	boiling water	1⅓ cups
1	tomato, finely chopped	1
½ cup	fresh parsley, finely chopped	½ cup
2	spring onions/scallions, finely chopped	2
¼ cup	fresh mint, finely chopped	¼ cup
	or 1 tbsp dried mint	
juice of	1 lemon	juice of
2 fl oz (60ml)	olive oil	¼ cup
	sea salt and freshly ground black pepper	
	Garnish	
a few	lettuce leaves	a few
1	tomato, sliced	1

1 Rinse the bulgar wheat under cold running water, then put it into a heatproof bowl.

2 Pour the boiling water over the wheat and leave it to soak for about 1 hour or until the water has been absorbed and the wheat is tender. Drain off and squeeze out any excess water.

3 Mix together all the chopped ingredients and stir them well into the wheat.

4 Blend together the lemon juice and oil and season to taste with sea salt and freshly ground black pepper. Pour this dressing over the salad and chill until you are ready to serve.

5 Serve the Tabbouleh on the lettuce leaves, decorated with the tomato slices.

Carrot and Pineapple Salad

Imperial (Metric)		American
4 medium	carrots	4 medium
½ small	fresh pineapple *or* ½ lb (225g/1 cup tinned/canned crushed pineapple plus juice	½ small
4-6 tbsp	orange juice	4-6 tbsp
1 tbsp	sunflower oil	1 tbsp
1	seedless orange *or* clementine	1
	mint *or* watercress leaves, to decorate	
1-2 tbsp	chopped walnuts/English walnuts	1-2 tbsp
2-3	dates, chopped	2-3

1 Grate (shred) the carrots and pineapple finely.
2 Mix them together with the orange juice and sunflower oil.
3 Peel and slice the orange horizontally, then cut each round in half or, if using a clementine, peel it and separate the segments.
4 Put them around the sides of your serving bowl in a decorative pattern.
5 Spoon the Carrot and Pineapple Salad carefully into the decorated bowl and decorate the top with the mint or watercress leaves and walnuts and dates.

Chick Pea Salad

Imperial (Metric)		American
½ lb (225g)	raw chick peas/garbanzo beans	1 cup
1-2	spring onion(s)/scallion(s), finely sliced	1-2
3	firm, ripe tomatoes, quartered	3
12	olives, stoned/pitted	12
1	small, ripe avocado	1
2 tbsp	fresh marjoram *or* chopped fresh parsley	2 tbsp
	Garnish	
1	free-range egg, hard-boiled/hard-cooked and sliced or mashed (optional)	1
3 tbsp	olive oil	3 tbsp
1 tbsp	lemon juice	1 tbsp
	sea salt, freshly ground black pepper and paprika	

1 Pick out and discard any discoloured or damaged chick peas (garbanzos), wash the chosen chick peas (garbanzos) well and soak them overnight or for 24 hours. Rinse them thoroughly, then put them into a pan full of fresh water, bring it to the boil and cook them for 10 minutes, rinse, fill the pan with fresh water, bring to the boil again and cook them until they are soft. Drain them, then leave them to cool.

2 Put the chick peas (garbanzos) into a salad bowl.

3 Add the spring onion (scallion) and tomato quarters to the bowl and mix them in, then scatter the olives over the top.

4 Peel and slice the avocado just before serving and arrange the slices attractively over the top of the salad. Sprinkle the marjoram or parsley over the salad. Arrange the egg, if using, over the salad.

5 Combine the olive oil and lemon juice and pour this dressing over the salad. Grind sea salt and black pepper and sprinkle paprika over the salad according to taste.

Salad Dressing

Imperial (Metric)		American
3 fl oz (90ml)	salad *or* olive oil	⅓ cup
2 tbsp	lemon juice *or* cider vinegar *or* 1 tbsp each	2 tbsp
¼ tsp	sea salt	¼ tsp
pinch	freshly ground black pepper	pinch
pinch	mustard powder (optional)	pinch
½ tsp	honey	½ tsp
2 tsp	chopped fresh parsley (optional)	2 tsp

1 Mix all the ingredients together very well and keep in the refrigerator until needed (it will keep for 2 weeks).
2 Add the parsley, if using, just before serving.

❖ 6 ❖
Desserts

❖ ―――――――――――――――――――――――――――――――― ❖
Dried Fruit Compote

Imperial (Metric)		American
1 lb (450g)	dried mixed fruit (peaches, pears, prunes, apples, etc.)	1 lb
⅔ pt (340ml)	apple *or* orange juice	1½ cups
2 tbsp	light demerara sugar	2 tbsp
2	oranges	2
1	pink grapefruit	1
	Garnish	
(4-7 fl oz) (115-200ml)	cream *or* yogurt	½-¾ cup
	handful nuts, chopped	

1 Soak the dried fruit overnight in the fruit juice and sugar in the refrigerator.
2 After soaking, transfer the fruit and remaining juices to a saucepan, bring it to the boil, then cook over a low heat for about 20-30 minutes until the fruit is soft.
3 Peel the oranges and grapefruit and cut them into small segments.
4 Stir them into the dried fruit mixture once it has cooked.
5 Leave it to cool, then chill the compote until you are ready to serve. Serve it cold with a generous spoonful of cream or yogurt on top and the nuts sprinkled over, if using.

Mango Fool

Imperial (Metric)		American
2 large	ripe mangoes	2 large
½ pt (285ml)	natural/unsweetened yogurt	1⅓ cups
2 tbsp	orange juice	2 tbsp
1½ tbsp	lemon juice	1½ tbsp
1½ tbsp	honey	1½ tbsp
	Garnish	
3 tbsp	chopped pistachio nuts	3 tbsp

1 Peel the mangoes and cut the fruit away from the stone/pit.
2 Purée the mango in a liquidizer or food processor. Add the rest of the ingredients (except the nuts) and blend them all well together.
3 Spoon into individual bowls or one serving bowl and chill for 3-4 hours. Decorate the top by sprinkling the pistachio nuts over just before serving.

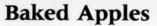

Baked Apples

Imperial (Metric)		American
4-6 medium	eating apples, washed	4-6 medium
3 tbsp	chopped nuts	3 tbsp
1 tbsp	chopped raisins	1 tbsp
½ tsp	ground cinnamon	½ tsp
4 tsp	honey	4 tsp
4 tsp	butter *or* polyunsaturated margarine	4 tsp

1 Preheat the oven to 350°F/180°C/gas mark 4.
2 Cut a thin slice off the top and remove the cores. Put them in an ovenproof casserole dish.
3 Combine the nuts, raisins and cinnamon and spoon the mixture into the hole where the core was.
4 Put a little honey on top of each filled apple, topped with a knob (small spoonful) of butter or margarine.
5 Pour a little water around the apples (about 115-200ml/4-7 fl oz/½-¾ cup) and bake in the preheated oven for about 30-40 minutes or until they are tender, then serve them warm, with cream, yogurt or custard.

Cheese Blintzes
(Stuffed Pancakes)

Imperial (Metric)		American
	Batter	
3	free-range eggs	3
¾ pt (425ml)	water and milk, mixed together	2 cups
6 oz (170g)	self-raising brown/wholewheat flour	1½ cups
½ tsp	baking powder	½ tsp
	vegetable oil, for frying	

	Cheese filling	
1	free-range egg	1
1-2 tbsp	creamy milk	1-2 tbsp
1 lb (450g)	cream cheese	2 cups
	sea salt	
1-2 tbsp	light demerara sugar	1-2 tbsp
2 tbsp	wholemeal/whole wheat flour	2 tbsp

1 First make the batter. Beat together the eggs and the water and milk mixture until frothy.

2 Sift the flour into a bowl together with the baking powder, then gradually add and beat it into the egg mixture until it has all been added and you have a smooth batter. Set it aside.

3 Now make the cheese filling. Beat together the egg and milk and then add the remaining ingredients, mixing them together well.

4 Preheat the oven to 350°F/180°C/gas mark 4.

5 Wipe a small frying pan (skillet) with kitchen paper (paper towel) dipped in a little vegetable oil and heat the pan.

6 Pour in sufficient batter to cover the pan thinly and cook, shaking it from time to time to prevent it sticking, until it is done. Cook the other side in the same way, then put it on kitchen paper (paper towels).

7 Repeat the process until all the batter has been used.

8 Fill each Blintz with a tablespoon or so of the filling, roll it up, folding in the ends and put them in a greased ovenproof casserole dish.

9 Dot the tops with butter or margarine and bake them in the preheated oven for about 30-40 minutes or until they are golden brown. Serve hot with yogurt or cinnamon and sugar, or apple sauce.

❖ Apple Crêpes ❖

Imperial (Metric)		American
	Apple filling	
6	Golden Delicious apples	6
2 tbsp	polyunsaturated margarine	2 tbsp
2 tbsp	orange juice	2 tbsp
2 tbsp	strawberry jam	2 tbsp
	Batter	
2	free-range eggs	2
1 tbsp	vegetable oil	1 tbsp
½ pt (285ml)	milk	1⅓ cups
½ pt (285ml)	water	1⅓ cups
6 oz (170g)	self-raising brown/wholewheat flour	1½ cups
pinch	sea salt	pinch
2 tsp	grated orange rind	2 tsp
2 tbsp	light demerara sugar	2 tbsp
	vegetable oil, as required	

1 Prepare the apple filling first. Peel and finely grate (shred) the apples.
2 Put the apple, margarine and orange juice into a saucepan and cook over a medium heat until the apple has softened.
3 Mix in the strawberry jam and add a little more orange juice if the mixture is too dry. Keep it warm.
4 Now make the batter for the crêpes.
5 Beat the eggs well, add the oil, milk and water and beat them until they are well combined.
6 Sift the flour into a separate bowl and add it slowly, a tablespoon at a time, to the egg mixture beating it in well.
7 Mix in the salt, orange rind and sugar.
8 Lightly oil a heavy frying pan (skillet) and heat it over a medium heat.
9 Pour the crêpe batter into a jug and pour a little at a time into the heated pan, swirling it to spread the mixture very thinly over the bottom of the pan, and fry it lightly on both sides for a few minutes, until it has cooked through.
10 Oil the frying pan (skillet) lightly before cooking each crêpe.

11 Stack the cooked crêpes and hand round the apple filling, so each person fills and rolls up their own crêpes.
12 Serve with yogurt or whipped cream.

 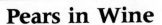

Pears in Wine

Imperial (Metric)		American
4	ripe pears	4
4 tbsp	chopped dates *or* raisins	4 tbsp
4 tbsp	finely chopped walnuts/English walnuts	4 tbsp
2 tsp	ground cinnamon	2 tsp
2 tsp	raw cane sugar	2 tsp
	polyunsaturated margarine *or* butter	
¼ pt (140ml)	sweet red wine	⅔ cup
¼ pt (140ml)	hot water	⅔ cup

1 Preheat the oven to 350°F/180°C/gas mark 4.
2 Peel and halve the pears, then neatly remove the cores. Place the pears in a greased ovenproof dish, cut side upwards.
3 Fill each pear half with the dates or raisins and walnuts. Sprinkle the cinnamon and sugar over the filling and pears and dot them with the margarine or butter.
4 Mix together the wine and water and pour the mixture over the pears and fillings and into the dish.
5 Cover and bake in the preheated oven for 20-30 minutes or until the pears are tender.
6 Serve them warm or cool with whipped cream or yogurt.

Russian Berry Kissel

Imperial (Metric)		American
1 lb (455g)	mixed berries (strawberries, raspberries, blackberries or cherries), washed and any pips/seeds removed	1 lb
¾ pt (425ml)	water	2 cups
2 oz (55g)	demerara sugar	⅓ cup
2 tsp	lemon juice	2 tsp
1 tbsp	blackcurrant juice	1 tbsp
2 tbsp	arrowroot	2 tbsp
2 tbsp	sweet red wine	2 tbsp
	Garnish	
4-6 tbsp	cream *or* yogurt	4-6 tbsp
a few	berries	a few

1 Simmer the fruit in the water, sugar, lemon juice and blackcurrant juice until they are soft.
2 Separate the fruit from the cooking liquid, reserving the juices and purée the fruit by hand or in a liquidizer or food processor.
3 Mix the arrowroot with a little water and the wine to form a thin, creamy liquid.
4 Slowly add some of the reserved hot fruit juice to this liquid, stirring all the time.
5 Combine the liquid with the puréed fruit and cook over a low heat, stirring until it thickens.
6 Serve cold, decorated with the cream or yogurt and the berries.

Strawberry Ice

Imperial (Metric)		American
1 lb (455g)	strawberries, washed and hulled	1 lb
3 fl oz (90ml)	unset honey	⅓ cup
½ pt (285ml)	orange juice	1⅓ cups
½ pt (285ml)	milk	1⅓ cups
2 tbsp	lemon juice	2 tbsp
1 tbsp	liqueur (optional)	1 tbsp
½ pt	cream	1⅓ cups
1 tbsp	raw cane sugar	1 tbsp

1 Mash the strawberries very well with the honey. Add the orange juice, milk and lemon juice and mix them together very well.
2 Spoon the mixture into a shallow freezeproof container and put this in the freezer. After 3-4 hours, when it is half frozen, take it out of the freezer and beat it very well, until the mixture is smooth. Add the liqueur at this point, if using.
3 Whip the cream and add the sugar, beating it in well.
4 Combine the beaten strawberry mixture with the whipped cream, beating it just enough to mix them well together.
5 Refreeze.
6 Remove it about 30 minutes before you are ready to serve.

Tapuzim
(Orange Surprise)

Imperial (Metric)		American
½ pt (285ml)	water	1⅓ cups
2 oz (55g)	light demerara sugar	⅓ cup
4 large	sweet oranges	4 large
1-2 tbsp	brandy *or* apricot liqueur	1-2 tbsp

1 Gently heat the water and sugar together and simmer the mixture for about 10 minutes.
2 Peel 1 orange very finely, taking care not to cut any of the white pith. Finely slice the peel and add it to the simmering syrup.
3 Peel the other 3 oranges, cutting away the pith. Cut the pith from the first orange.
4 Slice the oranges and remove any pips/small seeds and arrange the slices in a dish.
5 Add the brandy or apricot liqueur to the syrup and peel. Remove the pan from the stove and pour the syrup over the sliced oranges. Turn the slices to moisten them all over with it. Let it cool then chill.
6 Serve chilled or, alternatively, heat it through gently and serve it hot.

Cherry and Lychee Delight

Imperial (Metric)		American
1 lb (455g)	cherries, fresh *or* tinned/canned	1 lb
½ lb (225g)	lychees, fresh, peeled and stoned/pitted *or* tinned/canned	½ lb
2 tbsp	polyunsaturated margarine	2 tbsp
⅓ pt (200ml)	orange juice	¾ cup
2 tbsp	honey	2 tbsp
1 tsp	grated lemon rind	1 tsp
2 fl oz (60ml) or to taste	sweet red wine *or* Sabra liqueur	¼ cup or less or to taste
¼ tsp	ground cinnamon	¼ tsp

1 Preheat the oven to 325°F/170°C/gas mark 3.
2 Arrange the cherries and lychees in an attractive ovenproof casserole dish.
3 Melt the margarine in a saucepan, mix in the remaining ingredients and pour the mixture over the fruit in the dish.
4 Bake in the preheated oven for 20-30 minutes until the fruit is hot. Be careful not to overcook it.
5 Serve the dish warm with yogurt, fromage frais or ice-cream.

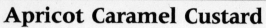

Apricot Caramel Custard

Imperial (Metric)		American
18	plump, dried apricots	18
	Caramel	
4 oz (115g)	light demerara sugar	⅔ cup
	Custard	
1 pt (570ml)	milk	2½ cups
2-3 tbsp	light demerara sugar	2-3 tbsp
2 tbsp	margarine	2 tbsp
3	free-range eggs	3
1 tsp	vanilla essence/extract	1 tsp

1   Pour boiling water over the dried apricots and leave them to soak for about 10 minutes.
2   Preheat the oven to 375°F/190°C/gas mark 5 and put a deep, ovenproof casserole dish in the oven.
3   Now make the caramel. Spread the sugar over the bottom of a heavy frying pan (skillet) and heat it until the sugar melts and liquidizes, but does not burn.
4   Remove the warmed casserole dish from the oven and pour the liquid sugar caramel into it, covering the bottom of the dish evenly.
5   Now make the custard. Heat the milk in a saucepan gently (do not boil) with the sugar and the margarine.
6   Meanwhile beat the eggs gently for a minute. Add the vanilla essence.
7   Pour some of the hot milk mixture over the eggs and mix it in well. Return this mixture to the milk mixture on the cooker, and stir until it just heats up again, (do not let it boil).
8   Remove the apricots from the hot water and arrange them over the caramelized sugar in the casserole dish.
9   Pour the custard over the apricots.
10 Put the casserole dish into a large ovenproof dish that has been lined with a small cloth and half-filled with hot water.
11 Bake in the pre-heated oven for 30-40 minutes until the top is golden brown.

12 Eat this dish warm or let it cool and chill until required, but remove it from the refrigerator and let it stand for about 30 minutes before eating.

Fruit Whip

Imperial (Metric)		American
½ lb (225g)	dried fruit (e.g. prunes, apricots, peaches)	1½ cups
⅓ pt (200ml)	water and orange juice, mixed	¾ cup
2 tsp	lemon juice	2 tsp
2 tbsp	honey	2 tbsp
½ pt (285ml)	natural/unsweetened yogurt	1⅓ cups
	Garnish	
4-6 tbsp	natural/unsweetened yogurt	4-6 tbsp
handful	walnuts/English walnuts, pecans or pistachios, chopped	handful

1 Wash the fruit well and remove the stones (pits) from prunes, if you are using them.
2 Boil the water and orange juice mixture together with the lemon juice and pour the mixture over the fruit. Leave it to soak overnight in a covered bowl.
3 Transfer the soaked fruit to a saucepan and cook it gently until it is soft, then leave it to cool.
4 Purée the fruit, together with the cooking liquid and honey, in a liquidizer or food processor.
5 Add the yogurt, mixing it in well.
6 Spoon the whip into a serving bowl or individual glass dishes, chill for 3-4 hours, then decorate with the yogurt and chopped nuts.

Sabra Gleeda
(Ice-cream)

Imperial (Metric)		American
2	free-range eggs	2
6 oz (170g)	light demerara sugar	1 cup
⅔ pt (340ml)	milk	1½ cups
½ pt (285ml)	double/heavy cream	1⅓ cups
¼ pt (140ml)	single/light cream	⅔ cup
2 tsp	liqueur *or* natural vanilla flavouring/extract	2 tsp
handful	nuts, chopped	handful
a little	chocolate *or* carob, grated/shredded	a little

1 Separate the egg yolks from the whites. Beat the egg whites until they are stiff and glossy, then set them to one side.
2 Combine the sugar and milk and beat them together well for about 10 minutes.
3 Pour both creams into the milk mixture and beat again for about 5 minutes. Add the liqueur or vanilla and the egg yolks, beating them in well.
4 Combine the beaten egg whites with the milk mixture and beat for about 5 minutes. Spoon the mixture into a shallow freezerproof container and freeze for about 3-4 hours.
5 Remove the container from the freezer, beat the mixture very well, mix in the nuts and chocolate or carob and refreeze. Remove the ice-cream from the freezer 30 minutes before serving it.

Note
In this recipe the eggs are not cooked.

❖ 7 ❖
Cakes and baked treats

❖

Sugariyot Sumsum
(Sesame Bites)

Imperial (Metric)		American
½ lb (250g)	sesame seeds	2 cups
1 oz (30g)	chopped almonds	¼ cup
6 oz (170g)	honey	½ cup
3 oz (85g)	demerara sugar	½ cup
	sunflower oil, for greasing	

1 Lay the sesame seeds and almonds on a lightly greased baking sheet and toast them in a 450°F/230°C/gas mark 8 oven for a few minutes, taking care not to burn them.
2 Oil a large bowl and put the toasted sesame seeds and nuts into it.
3 Heat the honey and sugar in a saucepan and boil the mixture for a few minutes after the sugar has melted, stirring it with a long-handled spoon, then pour it over the sesame seeds and almonds, stirring them in well.
4 Cut some greaseproof (waxed) paper to fit a baking sheet and brush it lightly with oil.
5 As the mixture is very hot, wear rubber kitchen gloves, moisten them and press the mixture onto the baking sheet in an even layer.
6 When it has cooled, turn the baking sheet over onto a flat surface, peel off the paper and break into bite-sized pieces.
7 The bites keep well in an air-tight container.
8 Serve them with coffee.

Cheesecake

Makes one 8 by 10 in (20.5 by 25.5 cm) cheesecake

Imperial (Metric)		American
½ lb (225g)	digestive biscuits/Graham crackers	½ lb
4 oz (115g)	polyunsaturated margarine	½ cup
3	free-range eggs	3
4 oz (115g)	fine, soft raw cane sugar	⅔ cup
1 lb (455g)	low-fat curd/cottage cheese, mashed	1 lb
½ lb (225g)	medium-fat cream cheese	½ lb
2 oz (55g)	polyunsaturated margarine, melted	¼ cup
2 tbsp	milk	2 tbsp
2 tsp	custard powder (optional)	2 tsp
1 tsp	vanilla essence (extract)	1 tsp

1 Put the digestive biscuits (Graham crackers) in a plastic bag and pound them with the end of a rolling pin to form crumbs. Melt the 4 oz (115g/½ cup) margarine, then stir it well into the biscuit crumbs until it is evenly distributed.
2 Press this mixture into the bottom of a greased ovenproof quiche dish and chill while you make the cheese mixture.
3 Preheat the oven to 350°F/180°C/gas mark 4.
4 Separate the eggs and beat the whites until they are firm, but not dry, with 2 tablespoons of the sugar then set the mixture to one side.
5 Beat the cheeses, egg yolks, 2 oz (55g/¼ cup) of melted margarine, the rest of the sugar, the milk, custard powder, if using, and the vanilla together. Beat the mixture well until it is smooth and creamy.
6 Fold in the beaten egg whites, gently with a metal spoon until they are well combined with the cheese mixture.
7 Spoon the mixture onto the crumb base and smooth the top.
8 Bake the cheesecake in the preheated oven for about 30 minutes or until it is golden brown.
9 Switch the oven off and leave the cheesecake in the oven for 30-40 minutes to prevent it sinking.
10 Serve the cheesecake warm or at room temperature or chill until needed.

Apple Farfel Tart

Makes one 8 × 10 in (20.5 × 25.5cm) tart

Imperial (Metric)		American
	Pastry	
4 oz (115g)	butter *or* polyunsaturated margarine	½ cup
4 oz (115g)	light demerara sugar	⅔ cup
1 tbsp	sunflower oil	1 tbsp
1	free-range egg, beaten	1
½ lb (225g)	wholemeal/whole wheat flour	2 cups
2 tbsp	ground nuts	2 tbsp
	Filling	
1 tbsp	smooth apricot jam/jelly	1 tbsp
1 tbsp	demerara sugar	1 tbsp
1½ tbsp	water	1½ tbsp
4 large	eating apples, peeled and thinly sliced	4 large

1 First make the pastry. Cream the butter or margarine, sugar and oil together.
2 Add the beaten egg and mix it well in.
3 Slowly add the flour and the ground nuts, mixing them in.
4 Knead the mixture lightly to make a soft but firm dough.
5 Take half the pastry and press it into a greased pie dish, covering the sides of the dish too.
6 Reserve the other half of the pastry for the Farfel topping.
7 Preheat the oven to 375°F/190°C/gas mark 5.
8 Now make the filling. Make a syrup by stirring the jam (jelly), sugar and water in a saucepan over a low heat.
9 Gently poach the apple slices in the syrup until they are tender.
10 Drain the cooked apples and spread them in the pastry case (shell).
11 Grate the reserved dough (add a little more flour if it is too soft to grate) and spread this over the apples.
12 Bake in the preheated oven for approximately 30 minutes until the top is golden brown.
13 Serve the pie warm with cream or custard, or cold with ice-cream.

Walnut Tart

Makes one 9-10-in (23-25.5-cm) tart

Imperial (Metric)		American
	Pastry	
3 oz (85g)	polyunsaturated margarine	⅓ cup
4 oz (115g)	self-raising brown/wholewheat flour	1 cup
1 tbsp	sunflower oil	1 tbsp
½ tsp	baking powder	½ tsp
1	free-range egg	1
	Filling	
3 oz (85g)	polyunsaturated margarine	⅓ cup
1½ tbsp	sunflower oil	1½ tbsp
4 tbsp	water	4 tbsp
3-4 tbsp	honey	3-4 tbsp
1 tsp	vanilla essence/extract	1 tsp
pinch	salt	pinch
1 tbsp	wholemeal/whole wheat flour	1 tbsp
½ lb (225g)	walnut/English walnut pieces	½ lb

1 Cut the margarine into the flour, then blend it in with the finger tips until the mixture resembles fine breadcrumbs. Stir in the oil and baking powder.
2 Beat the egg then blend it into the pastry. Knead the dough slightly.
3 Press the pastry into a large, greased pie dish (the dough is sticky, so a sprinkling of flour will make handling easier). Chill it while you make the filling.
4 Preheat the oven to 400°F/200°C/gas mark 6.
5 Now make the filling. Boil together the margarine, oil, water, honey and vanilla.
6 Blend the flour with a little water and pour a little of the hot margarine mixture into it. Stir them together and pour the flour mixture into the saucepan. Heat the mixture slowly, stirring well, and remove the pan from the heat when the mixture begins to boil.
7 Spread the walnut pieces over the bottom of the pastry case (shell).

8 Pour the margarine mixture over the walnuts.
9 Bake in the preheated oven for about 20-30 minutes or until the pastry is cooked through.

Variation:
Spread 4 tablespoons of soaked raisins onto pastry case before you add the walnuts.

Hungarian Cherry Cake

Makes one 8 × 10 in (20.5 × 25.5cm) cake

Imperial (Metric)		American
3	free-range eggs	3
4 oz (115g)	light demerara sugar	⅔ cup
6 oz (170g)	polyunsaturated margarine	⅔ cup
	or softened butter	
6 oz (170g)	self-raising brown/wholewheat flour	1½ cups
1 lb (450g)	sweet red cherries	1 lb
	(fresh or tinned/canned)	
	raw cane sugar, for sprinkling	

1 Separate the eggs.
2 Beat half the sugar with the 3 egg whites until the mixture is stiff.
3 Cream the remaining sugar with the margarine or butter, then beat in the egg yolks, a little at a time.
4 Preheat the oven to 350°F/180°C/gas mark 4.
5 Fold the egg white mixture gently into the butter and egg yolk mixture using a metal spoon.
6 Sift the flour to make it lighter and tip the bran back into it. Gently fold the flour into the egg mixture a little at a time, using a metal spoon.
7 Pour the mixture into a greased, rectangular, paper-lined tin/pan.
8 If using fresh cherries, remove the stones/pits; if using tinned cherries, drain them. Press them into the batter.
9 Bake in the preheated oven for about 30 minutes or until the cake is golden brown.
10 Sprinkle a few teaspoons of raw cane sugar over the cake and serve it warm or cold.

Lekach
(Honey Cake)

Makes one 9-10-in (23-25.5-cm) cake

Imperial (Metric)		American
2	free-range eggs	2
1 lb (455g)	honey	1¼ cups
¼ pt (140ml)	sunflower oil	⅔ cup
4 oz (115g)	light demerara sugar	⅔ cup
1 tsp	ground cinnamon	1 tsp
¼ tsp	ground ginger	¼ tsp
¾ lb (340g)	self-raising brown/wholewheat flour	3 cups
½ pt (285ml)	water and orange juice, mixed together	1⅓ cups
2 tsp	bicarbonate of soda/baking soda	2 tsp
	Icing (frosting) (optional)	
2 oz (55g)	polyunsaturated margarine	¼ cup
2 tbsp	honey	2 tbsp
1 tsp	lemon juice	2 tsp
as required	icing sugar	as required

1 Grease a 9-10-in (23-25.5-cm round cake tin (pan) and preheat the oven to 350°F/180°C/gas mark 4.
2 Beat the eggs, honey, oil, sugar, cinnamon and ginger together well.
3 Add the flour, a little at a time, beating the mixture well after each addition.
4 Boil the water and juice mixture, add the bicarbonate of soda (baking soda) and pour this gently into the cake mixture. Beat the mixture lightly until the hot mixture has been well combined with the cake mixture.
5 Pour the cake mixture into the prepared cake tin (pan) and bake in the preheated oven for about 1 hour but after about 40 minutes, cover the top of the cake with greaseproof paper to prevent it burning. Check if it is cooked by inserting a skewer: if it comes out clean, then the cake is done.

6 Now make the icing (frosting), if using. Melt the margarine, stir in the honey and lemon juice, then blend in sufficient icing sugar until the mixture is of a dropping consistency. Add a few teaspoons of hot water, then spread it over the cake.
7 Serve Lekach sliced and buttered if not using the icing (frosting).

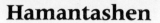

Hamantashen
(Fruity Triangles)

Makes about 20

Imperial (Metric)		American
	Pastry	
2	free-range eggs	2
4 oz (115g)	raw cane sugar	½ cup
2 fl oz (60ml)	sunflower oil	¼ cup
1 tbsp	orange juice	1 tbsp
1 tsp	lemon juice	1 tsp
¾ lb (340g)	self-raising brown/wholewheat flour	3 cups
1 tsp	baking powder	1 tsp
	Filling	
½ lb (225g)	prunes, stoned/pitted	½ lb
½ lb (225g)	raisins	½ lb
2 oz (55g)	raw cane sugar	¼ cup
1-2 tbsp	lemon juice	1-2 tbsp

1 First make the pastry. Beat the eggs and sugar together well until the mixture becomes light and creamy.
2 Add the oil and juices, beating them in well.
3 Slowly add the flour and baking powder.
4 Knead the dough lightly, adding a little more flour if it is too sticky to knead, but the pastry should be soft.
5 Now make the filling. Blend the filling ingredients in a liquidizer or food processor until you have a thick paste. Taste and adjust the sweetness or sharpness according to your preference.
6 Divide the pastry in half or into thirds and roll each piece out to about an ⅛ in (3mm) thickness. Cut the pastry into 4-in (10-cm) squares and place a tablespoon of the filling in the middle of each square. Fold a corner over the filling and align it with the corner on the opposite side to form a triangle and pinch the edges together in the middle. Put them on a greased baking sheet and bake them in the preheated oven for about 10-20 minutes until they are golden brown.

Toasted Mandelbrot
(Almond Biscuits)
Makes about 50

Imperial (Metric)		American
3	free-range eggs	3
½ lb (225g)	demerara sugar	1⅓ cups
4 fl oz (115ml)	sunflower oil	½ cup
2 tsp	vanilla essence/extract	2 tsp
¾ lb (340g)	self-raising brown/wholewheat flour	3 cups
pinch	sea salt	pinch
2½ tsp	baking powder	2½ tsp
½ tsp	ground cinnamon	½ tsp
½ lb (225g)	chopped almonds *or* mixed nuts	1½ cups
	grated/shredded orange rind (optional)	

1 Preheat the oven to 400°F/200°C/gas mark 6.
2 Beat the eggs very well.
3 Add the sugar gradually, beating it into the eggs well. Add the oil and vanilla, also beating them in well.
4 Add the flour gradually, also mixing in the salt, baking powder and the cinnamon.
5 Stir in the nuts. The dough should now be neither too soft nor sticky so add a little extra flour if necessary. Knead it very gently on a floured surface.
6 Divide the dough into 4 portions and roll out each one until it is about 3 in (8 cm) across, ½ in (1.25 cm) thick and about 10 in (25 cm) long. Put the biscuits on well greased and lightly floured baking sheets.
7 Bake them in the preheated oven for about 20 minutes until they have risen slightly and are just golden brown rather than browned. Leave the oven on.
8 Remove the biscuits from the baking sheets and leave them to cool slightly.
9 Cut each biscuit into ¾-in (2-cm) wide slices and place them cut sides up on the baking sheets.
10 Put them back in the oven for about 5-10 minutes to toast. Turn them over halfway through the cooking time to toast each side.

❖ Mrs Cooper's Wholemeal Challah

Makes 2 loaves and 4 rolls

Imperial (Metric)		American
3 tsp	dried yeast	3 tsp
1 tsp	light demerara sugar	1 tsp
13 fl oz (370ml)	very warm water	1½ cups plus 2 tbsp
1 lb (455g)	wholemeal/whole wheat flour	4 cups
½ lb (225g)	strong plain/bread flour	2 cups
2 tsp	sea salt	2 tsp
2 tbsp	light demerara sugar	2 tbsp
4 fl oz (115ml)	sunflower oil	½ cup
1	free-range egg	1
	For glazing	
1	free-range egg, beaten	1
	sesame seeds	

1 Mix the yeast with the 1 teaspoon sugar and 3 fl oz (90 ml/⅓ cup) of the very warm water in a measuring jug and set the mixture to one side until it has doubled its bulk (it has reached the 6 fl oz/170ml/⅔ cup mark).

2 Into a bowl, put the flours, salt, sugar, oil and one egg, then, when the yeast mixture is ready, add it, together with the remaining water (which still needs to be very warm) and mix them together to form a soft dough.

3 Start kneading the dough by hand or using a food processor until it is smooth and leaves the sides of the bowl. As flour varies in absorbency, it may be necessary to add a little more very warm water to make the dough smooth.

4 Cover the bowl with a cloth and leave the dough to rise in a warm place until it has doubled in size.

5 Knock it back (punch it down) and knead it for just a minute to reduce it to its original size and form it into a smooth, round ball.

6 Form it into a long roll and divide this into 12 equal pieces (each should weigh about 3 oz/85g). Roll the pieces to form strands about 5-7 in (12.5-18 cm) long.

7 Using 4 of the strands, plait them together attractively.

Repeat with 4 more strands so you have 2 Challah loaves, then twist each of the remaining 4 strands to make 4 Challah rolls.

8 Preheat the oven to 350°F/180°C/gas mark 4.

9 Leave them all to rest (stand) in a warm place for 30-45 minutes to rise. Glaze with the beaten egg, sprinkle the sesame seeds over them and bake on the middle shelf in the preheated oven for about 30 minutes until they are golden brown.

Note
The Challah dough may be made the night before and left to rise overnight, proceeding from step 5 the next day.

❖ ──────────────────────────────────── ❖

Mom's Crumpets

Makes about 24 crumpets

Imperial (Metric)		American
1 size 1	free-range egg	1 extra large
1 generous tbsp	light demerara sugar	1 heaped tbsp
8 fl oz (240ml)	water and milk, mixed together	1 cup
2 heaped tbsp	self-raising brown/wholewheat flour, sifted	2 heaped tbsp
3 heaped tbsp	plain/all-purpose white flour, sifted	3 heaped tbsp
2 tsp	baking powder	2 tsp
pinch	sea salt	pinch
1 tsp	polyunsaturated margarine sunflower oil, for frying	1 tsp

1 Beat the egg and sugar together until the mixture becomes light and creamy.
2 Add the water and milk, beating the mixture in well.
3 Add the flours, a little at a time, mixing them in well. Add the baking powder and salt, stirring them in well.
4 Melt the margarine and mix it into the crumpet mixture.
5 Over a medium heat, place a lightly oiled frying pan (skillet) and drop the crumpet batter a tablespoon at a time on to the pan. When the top of the crumpet bubbles, after a few minutes, turn the crumpet over and cook it on the other side.
6 Oil the frying pan (skillet) very lightly between each batch of crumpets, rubbing it over the pan with brown paper.
7 Serve the crumpets warm, buttered, with jam/jelly or honey.

Note
Make double quantities if you are expecting guests as these crumpets go very quickly!

❖ 8 ❖
Passover

Take care to use only 'Supervised for Passover' ingredients during Passover.

Vegetable Soup

Imperial (Metric)		American
1 large	ripe tomato, skinned and chopped	1 large
2	carrots, grated/shredded	2
1 small	onion, chopped	1 small
1	leek, chopped	1
2	sticks celery/celery stalks, chopped	2
1 small	parsnip, chopped	1 small
1	potato, chopped	1
6-8 cups	water	6-8 cups
2 tbsp	chopped fresh parsley	2 tbsp
	sea salt and freshly ground black pepper	
1	vegetable stock/bouillon cube (optional)	1
1 tbsp	tomato purée/paste	1 tbsp

1 Simmer the vegetables gently in the water for approximately 1-1½ hours or until the vegetables are soft.
2 Add the parsley, season to taste with sea salt and freshly ground black pepper. Add the cube at this point if using.
3 Serve with Matzo Kleis (see page 154) or Kneidlach (see page 52), but use only authorized Passover ingredients.

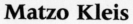

Matzo Kleis
(Matzo Meal Soup Dumplings)

Makes about 12–14

Imperial (Metric)		American
2	matzos	2
1 small	onion, finely chopped	1 small
2 tbsp	vegetable oil	2 tbsp
1 tbsp	chopped fresh parsley	1 tbsp
2 tbsp	ground almonds	2 tbsp
pinch	ground ginger	pinch
2 tsp	ground cinnamon	2 tsp
	sea salt and freshly ground black pepper	
1 oz (30g)	Matzo meal, fine, as required	¼ cup
2	free-range eggs, beaten	2

1 Leave the matzos to soak in a little cold water until they are soft. When they are quite soft, remove them and squeeze out the excess water. Mash the matzos well.
2 Fry the onion in the oil until they have softened and are golden brown.
3 Add onions with the cooking oil to the mashed matzos.
4 Add the parsley, almonds, ginger, cinnamon and season to taste with sea salt and freshly ground black pepper. Mix them in well then mix in the eggs.
5 Stir in just enough of the matzo meal to make a firm, but not hard, consistency. Chill the mixture for about an hour.
6 From the mixture make small balls, about the size of a large walnut, and dip them into the matzo meal.
7 Boil the balls gently in salted water for about 20 minutes, then drain them and serve them with soup.
8 Alternatively, the cooked balls can be put in a vegetable casserole and baked for about 30-40 minutes. They would make a filling addition to the Mushroom and Aubergine Bake (see page 171) or Israeli Casserole (see page 165), for example.

Charoset

Imperial (Metric)		American
3	Golden Delicious apples	3
6 tbsp	finely ground hazelnuts and almonds, mixed together	6 tbsp
2 tsp	ground cinnamon	2 tsp
2 tbsp	sweet red Kiddush wine	2 tbsp

1 Peel and grate/shred the apples finely into a bowl.
2 Mix in the hazelnuts and almonds and cinnamon.
3 Add the wine and mix all the ingredients together well.
4 Cover the bowl and chill the Charoset until you need it for the Seder.

Note
Charoset is eaten at the Seder meals and is a reminder of the mortar used in the building work before the Exodus from Egypt.

Vegetable Roast

Imperial (Metric)		American
1 medium	aubergine/eggplant	1 medium
	sea salt and freshly ground black pepper	
1 medium	onion, chopped	1 medium
2	cloves garlic, chopped	2
	vegetable oil, for frying	
3	carrots, scraped and chopped	3
3 small	courgettes/zucchini, chopped	3 small
3 medium	tomatoes, chopped	3 medium
1 tbsp	tomato purée/paste	1 tbsp
4-6 tbsp	matzo meal	4-6 tbsp
1	free-range egg, beaten	1
2-3	parboiled potatoes, sliced	2-3
1 tbsp	paprika	1 tbsp

1 Slice the aubergine (eggplant), layer them in a colander or large plate, salting each layer and leave them for 30 minutes or until the bitter juices have oozed out. Then rinse them well, pat them dry and chop the slices into smaller pieces.
2 Fry the onion and garlic in a little oil for a few minutes.
3 Add the carrot, courgette (zucchini), tomato and aubergine (eggplant).
4 Stir the vegetables together and cook them over a low heat for about 20 minutes. Add a little water, if the mixture becomes too dry. Check that the carrot has softened.
5 Preheat the oven to 350°F/180°C/gas mark 4.
6 Purée the vegetables briefly in a liquidizer or food processor or mash them by hand, but the mixture must be a rough, rather than smooth purée.
7 Add the matzo meal, season well with the sea salt and freshly ground black pepper and taste. Mix in the beaten egg.
8 Spoon the mixture into a greased, ovenproof casserole dish and arrange the potato slices over the top of the mixture. Sprinkle the paprika over the top.
9 Bake in the preheated oven for about 30-40 minutes until the topping is golden brown.

Gedempte Gemüse mit Nisslach
(Vegetable and Nut Casserole)

Imperial (Metric)		American
1½ oz (45g)	polyunsaturated margarine	3 tbsp
2 large	carrots, finely grated/shredded	2 large
2	sticks celery/celery stalks, finely chopped	2
2 medium	onions, finely chopped	2 medium
2 oz (55g)	mushrooms, chopped	¾ cup
5 oz (140g)	ground mixed nuts	1 cup
1 tbsp	chopped fresh parsley	1 tbsp
2	tomatoes, skinned and chopped	2
4 oz (115g)	matzo meal	1 cup
2	free-range eggs, beaten	2
2 tbsp	tomato purée/paste	2 tbsp
	sea salt, freshly ground black pepper and paprika	
⅓ pt (200ml)	vegetable stock	¾ cup
4 tbsp	lemon juice	4 tbsp

1 Preheat the oven to 350°F/180°C/gas mark 4.
2 Melt the margarine and lightly fry the carrot, celery, onion and mushroom. Add a little oil if too dry.
3 Add the nuts, parsley and sauté for another 5-10 minutes.
4 Remove the pan from the heat, add the remaining ingredients and mix them in well. Transfer the mixture to a well-greased casserole dish.
5 Bake in the preheated oven for about 45 minutes, until it has cooked through.

Note
You can top the casserole with sliced, parboiled or mashed potatoes at the end of step 4, which will brown during baking.

Gravy

Imperial (Metric)		American
small piece	of onion	small piece
1	clove garlic	1
2 tbsp	butter *or* polyunsaturated margarine	2tbsp
1 tbsp	potato flour	1 tbsp
	sea salt, freshly ground black pepper and paprika	
10-14 fl oz (285-400ml)	hot vegetable stock (made with vegetable soup cube)	1¼-1¾ cups
1 tbsp	red wine (optional)	1 tbsp

1 Lightly sauté the onion and garlic in the butter or margarine. Remove the onion and garlic and take the fat off the heat.
2 Blend the potato flour and seasonings into the fat and return the pan to a low heat, browning the flour lightly.
3 Slowly add the hot stock, stirring all the time until all the stock has been incorporated and the gravy has thickened. Add the wine at this point, if using. Serve with Vegetable and Nut Casserole (see page 157), or other dishes of your choice.

Note
The gravy may be varied by adding chopped, sautéed mushrooms.

Goulash with Potato Kneidlach

Imperial (Metric)		American
	Goulash	
2 medium	onions, chopped	2 medium
1 small	green pepper, chopped	1 small
	vegetable oil, for frying	
2	cloves garlic, crushed/minced	2
1½ lb (675g)	courgettes/zucchini, washed and sliced	1½ lb

3-4	ripe tomatoes, skinned and chopped	3-4
1 tsp	paprika, or to taste	1 tsp
	sea salt and freshly ground black pepper	
1 tbsp	chopped fresh parsley	1 tbsp
10-14 fl oz (285-400ml)	hot vegetable stock	1¼-1¾ cups

Kneidlach mixture

2½ cups	grated/shredded potatoes, uncooked	2½ cups
1	onion, grated/shredded	1
2 oz (55g)	matzo meal	½ cup
1 tbsp	ground nuts	1 tbsp
1 tbsp	potato flour	1 tbsp
1	free-range egg	1
1-2 tsp	sea salt	1-2 tsp
	freshly ground black pepper	

1 Fry the onion and green pepper lightly in a little oil, together with the garlic.
2 Add the courgette (zucchini) to the onion and green pepper.
3 Add the tomato to the mixture. Stir in the paprika, season to taste with sea salt and freshly ground black pepper and add the parsley. Transfer the mixture to an ovenproof casserole dish.
4 Pour the hot stock over the vegetables.
5 Now make the Kneidlach mixture. Drain any liquid from the potato and add it to the vegetable stock in the goulash.
6 Combine the remaining ingredients, mixing them together well. Add more matzo meal if necessary to make a firm consistency.
7 Form the mixture into balls.
8 Put the Kneidlach balls on top of the mixture and cover the casserole dish.
9 Bake in the preheated oven (350°F/180°C/gas mark 4) for about 45 minutes. Remove the lid to allow the Kneidlach to brown for about 20 minutes.

Note
If time is short, use sliced parboiled potatoes to top the Goulash instead of the Kneidlach.

Aubergine Schnitzel in Lemon and Tomato Sauce

Imperial (Metric)		American
1 large	aubergine/eggplant	1 large
	sea salt, freshly ground black pepper,	
	paprika and onion salt	
1	free-range egg, beaten	1
4 oz (115g)	matzo meal	about 1 cup
	vegetable oil, for frying	
2 tsp	lemon juice	2 tsp
1 tbsp	tomato purée/paste	1 tbsp

1   Peel the aubergine (eggplant) and slice it lengthwise, cutting the slices in half across if they are very long. Layer the slices in a colander or large plate, salting each layer, and leave them for 30 minutes or until the bitter juices have oozed out. Rinse them well and pat them dry.
2   Season the matzo meal well with sea salt, freshly ground black pepper, paprika and onion salt.
3   Dip the aubergine (eggplant) slices first into the beaten egg, then into the seasoned matzo meal.
4   Preheat the oven to 325°F/170°C/gas mark 3.
5   Heat a little oil in a frying pan (skillet) and fry the aubergine (eggplant) slices briefly on both sides until they are golden brown.
6   Put the cooked slices in a casserole dish.
7   Cover the aubergine (eggplant) slices with hot water to which has been added ½ teaspoon sea salt, the lemon juice, and the tomato purée.
8   Bake, uncovered, in the preheated oven until most of the liquid has been absorbed, leaving a thick sauce.
9   Serve with roast potatoes and sautéed courgettes (zucchini), onions and tomatoes.

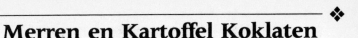

Merren en Kartoffel Koklaten
(Carrot and Potato Patties)

Imperial (Metric)		American
1 lb (455g)	carrots	1 lb
1 lb (455g)	potatoes	1 lb
2 medium	onions, chopped	2 medium
2	cloves garlic, crushed/minced	2
	vegetable oil, for frying	
	sea salt and freshly ground black pepper	
1 tsp	garlic salt	1 tsp
2 tsp	paprika	2 tsp
2-3 tbsp	tomato purée/paste	2-3 tbsp
2 tbsp	chopped fresh parsley	2 tbsp
1	free-range egg, beaten (optional)	1
2 oz (55g)	fine matzo meal, as required	½ cup

1 Peel and dice the carrots and potatoes, then boil or steam them together until they are tender.
2 Fry the onions and garlic in a little of the vegetable oil until they are golden brown.
3 Preheat the oven to 375°F/190°C/gas mark 5.
4 Mash the carrots and potatoes together well, season to taste with sea salt and freshly ground black pepper and mix in the garlic salt, paprika and tomato purée.
5 Add the fried onions and garlic and the oil in which they were fried. Mix them in well.
6 Add the parsley and the egg, if using.
7 Mix in enough matzo meal to make a firm consistency. Add more seasoning if desired.
8 Form the mixture into patties, brush them with oil and bake them on a greased baking sheet in the preheated oven for 30-45 minutes until they are crisp.

❖ Baked Peppers with Egg ❖

Imperial (Metric)		American
4 large	green peppers	4 large
1 medium	aubergine/eggplant	1 medium
	sea salt, freshly ground black pepper and paprika	
1 medium	onion, chopped	1 medium
	oil, for frying	
2	ripe tomatoes, chopped	2
2 tbsp	chopped fresh parsley	2 tbsp
4	parboiled potatoes, sliced	4
4	free-range eggs	4

1 Boil the peppers in lightly salted water for about 10 minutes.
2 Slice the aubergine (eggplant), layer the slices in a colander, or large plate, salt each layer and leave to stand for 30 minutes or until the bitter juices ooze out. Rinse them well, pat them dry and chop the slices into small pieces.
3 Sauté the onion in a little oil until it is golden brown. Add the aubergine (eggplant) and cook gently for about 15 minutes. Add the tomatoes and parsley, season to taste with sea salt, freshly ground black pepper and paprika and cook for a further 10 minutes.
4 Preheat the oven to 350°F/180°C/gas mark 4.
5 Slice each of the green peppers in half lengthwise and scoop out the seeds and ribs.
6 Place the pepper halves in a large, greased ovenproof casserole dish. Fill each cavity with the onion, aubergine (eggplant) and tomato mixture.
7 Arrange the potato slices around the filled peppers.
8 Beat the eggs with a little sea salt and freshly ground black pepper and pour them over the green peppers and potato slices.
9 Bake in the preheated oven for about 30-40 minutes until the filled peppers and potato slices are well cooked, then serve hot.

Nisslach Koklaten
(Nut Rissoles)

Imperial (Metric)		American
1 medium	onion, chopped	1 medium
1	clove garlic, crushed/minced	1
1	stick celery/celery stalk, chopped	1
2 oz (55g)	polyunsaturated margarine	¼ cup
2 tbsp	matzo meal	2 tbsp
	sea salt and freshly ground black pepper	
½ tsp	garlic salt	½ tsp
3 fl oz (90ml)	vegetable stock	⅓ cup
½ lb (225g)	ground hazelnuts *or* walnuts	2 cups
1 tbsp	chopped fresh parsley	1 tbsp
1 tbsp	lemon juice	1 tbsp
1 tbsp	tomato purée/paste	1 tbsp
1	free-range egg, beaten (optional)	1

1 Sauté the onion, garlic and celery in the margarine.
2 Add the matzo meal, season to taste with sea salt and freshly ground black pepper, add the garlic salt and stir well.
3 Preheat the oven to 350°F/180°C/gas mark 4.
4 Add the stock, nuts, parsley, lemon juice and tomato purée.
5 Stir all the ingredients together well and cook for about 5 minutes. Check the seasoning and adjust to taste if necessary. Add beaten egg at this point, if using.
6 Shape the mixture into rounds and put them on a greased baking sheet and bake in the preheated oven until they have browned.

❖ ———————————————————————————

Potato Pizzas

Makes two 7 by 11-in (18 by 28-cm) pizzas

Imperial (Metric)		American
	Base	
3-4 medium	potatoes, boiled or steamed	3-4 medium
2 oz (55g)	polyunsaturated margarine	¼ cup
3 oz (85g)	fine matzo meal	¾ cup
1 oz (30g)	potato flour	¼ cup
	sea salt, freshly ground black pepper and paprika	
	Filling	
1 medium	onion, finely chopped	1 medium
1	clove garlic, crushed/minced	1
	vegetable oil, for frying	
1 medium	carrot, grated/shredded	1 medium
2 ripe	tomatoes, skinned and chopped	2 ripe
2 tbsp	tomato purée/paste	2 tbsp
1 tbsp	chopped fresh parsley	1 tbsp
	sea salt, freshly ground black pepper and paprika	
4 oz (115g)	grated cheese	1 cup

1 Preheat the oven to 400°F/200°C/gas mark 5.
2 First make the pizza bases. Mash the potatoes by hand or in a liquidizer or food processor together with the margarine. Mix in the matzo meal, potato flour and season to taste with sea salt, freshly ground black pepper and paprika. Knead the dough lightly.
3 Lightly grease two 7 by 11-in (18 by 28-cm) tins (pans), divide the dough in half and roll each out to fit the pans. Lay the dough in the pans.
4 Bake them in the preheated oven for about 20-30 minutes and leave the oven on.
5 Meanwhile prepare the filling. Sauté the onion, garlic and grated carrots in a little oil until they have softened. Add the tomatoes, tomato purée, parsley and season to taste with sea salt, freshly ground black pepper and paprika.
6 Stir the mixture well and spread it over the baked pizza bases. Sprinkle the cheese over the top.

7 Bake the pizzas in the oven until the cheese has melted (about 15-20 minutes) and the topping is heated through.

Variation
Instead of cheese, top your pizzas with sautéed sliced mushrooms.

Israeli Casserole

Imperial (Metric)		American
1	aubergine/eggplant	1
	sea salt and freshly ground black pepper	
2	onions, chopped	2
1 small	green pepper, deseeded and chopped	1 small
1	clove garlic, crushed/minced	1
	vegetable oil, for frying	
4 medium	potatoes, parboiled in their skins, then peeled and diced	4 medium
½ pt (285ml)	hot vegetable stock	1⅓ cups
6-8 medium-sized	ripe tomatoes, skinned and chopped	6-8 medium-sized
1 tbsp	chopped fresh parsley	1 tbsp

1 Peel the aubergine (eggplant) taking as little of the flesh off with it as possible, cut the flesh into thick slices, layer them in a colander or large plate, salting each layer, and leave them for 30 minutes until the bitter juices have oozed out. Wash the slices well, pat them dry and then cut them into smaller pieces.
2 Sauté the onion, green pepper and garlic in a little oil for about 5 minutes.
3 Preheat the oven to 350°F/180°C/gas mark 4.
4 Add the aubergine (eggplant) and potato and sauté them until they have softened and are beginning to brown. Transfer them to an ovenproof casserole dish with a lid.
5 Pour the stock, tomato and parsley into the casserole. Season to taste with sea salt and freshly ground black pepper, cover and bake in the preheated oven for 30-45 minutes.

Cauliflower Koklaten
(Cauliflower Patties)

Imperial (Metric)		American
1 medium	cauliflower, washed and divided into florets	1 medium
1 small	onion, grated/shredded	1 small
	vegetable oil, for frying	
2 oz (55g)	chopped mixed nuts	½ cup
1 tbsp	chopped fresh parsley	1 tbsp
1½ tbsp	potato flour	1½ tbsp
1 tsp	paprika	1 tsp
	sea salt, freshly ground black pepper and a pinch sugar	
2	free-range eggs, beaten	2
1 tbsp	lemon juice	1 tbsp

1 Steam or boil the cauliflower until it is tender.
2 Fry the onion in a little vegetable oil until it is golden brown and has softened.
3 Combine the onion, together with the oil in which it was fried, with the nuts.
4 Mash the cooked cauliflower.
5 Mix together the cauliflower, nut mixture, parsley, potato flour, paprika, sea salt, freshly ground black pepper and sugar, the eggs and lemon juice.
6 Preheat the oven to 350°F/180°C/gas mark 4.
7 Chill the mixture for about 20 minutes then form it into patties.
8 Put them on a greased baking sheet and bake them in the preheated oven for about 30-45 minutes. Serve with cheese sauce (see page 169) or tomato gravy.
9 Alternatively, do not chill the mixture but put it in a greased casserole dish, smooth the top and bake as in step 8.

Beetroot Bake

Imperial (Metric)		American
1 medium	onion, finely chopped	1 medium
1	stick celery/celery stalk, chopped	1
1 tbsp	oil	1 tbsp
3 medium	beetroot/beet, grated/shredded	3 medium
2 medium	carrots, grated/shredded	2 medium
1	Granny Smith apple, grated/shredded	1
2 tbsp	chopped fresh parsley	2 tbsp
4 tbsp	matzo meal	4 tbsp
6 tbsp	lemon juice	6 tbsp
2 tbsp	tomato purée/paste	2 tbsp
	sea salt, freshly ground black pepper and paprika	
	Garnish	
2 tbsp	finely chopped fresh parsley	2 tbsp

1 Preheat the oven to 350°F/180°C/gas mark 4.
2 Lightly fry the onion and celery in the oil until they have softened.
3 Combine all the remaining ingredients in a large bowl, mixing them together thoroughly.
4 Spoon the mixture into a greased ovenproof casserole dish, pressing it down evenly.
5 Bake in the preheated oven for about 1 hour until it is cooked and the top has lightly browned.
6 Garnish with the finely chopped parsley before serving either hot or cold.

Baked Gefilte Patties

Imperial (Metric)		American
3 medium	potatoes, peeled	3 medium
2 medium	onions, finely chopped	2 medium
	vegetable oil, for frying	
1 large	aubergine/eggplant	1 large
2	cloves garlic, crushed/minced	2
2 tbsp	chopped fresh parsley	2 tbsp
	sea salt, freshly ground black pepper and paprika	
	matzo meal, as required	

1 Boil or steam the potatoes until they are tender, then put them to one side.
2 Preheat the oven to 425°F/220°C/gas mark 7.
3 Fry the onion in a little of the oil until they have turned a dark, golden brown colour.
4 Top and tail the aubergine (eggplant), slice it in half lengthwise, sprinkle the flesh with oil and place them on greased baking sheet, flesh sides down. Prick the skin in a few places with a fork.
5 Bake the aubergine (eggplant) in the preheated oven until the skin starts to shrivel and the flesh is soft (about 20-30 minutes). Scoop out the flesh when it has cooked. Turn the oven down to 350°F/180°C/gas mark 4.
6 Mash the potatoes, add the cooked onion, the aubergine (eggplant) flesh, garlic, parsley, season to taste with sea salt, freshly ground black pepper and paprika, then mix in sufficient matzo meal to make a firm (but not hard) consistency.
7 Wet your hands and shape tablespoonsful of the mixture into patties. Put the patties on oiled baking sheets and sprinkle each one with a little oil.
8 Bake them in the oven for 30 minutes until they are golden brown.
9 Serve them hot or cold with salads and horseradish (Chrain), which can be bought at most Jewish delicatessens.

Courgette and Leek Casserole

Imperial (Metric)		American
4 large	leeks	4 large
1½ lb (680g)	courgettes/zucchini, washed and sliced	1½ lb
	vegetable oil, for frying	
	sea salt and freshly ground black pepper	
	garlic salt	
	Cheese sauce	
1 oz (30g)	butter *or* polyunsaturated margarine	2½ tbsp
1 tbsp	potato flour	1 tbsp
½ pt (285ml)	milk and vegetable stock, mixed together	1⅓ cups
	sea salt and freshly ground black pepper	
½ tsp	ground nutmeg	½ tsp
2 oz (55g)	grated cheese	½ cup

1　First prepare the vegetables. Cut the leeks lengthwise and wash them very well under running cold water, then slice them thinly. Steam or boil them in a little water until they are tender.

2　Sauté the courgette (zucchini) in a little of the vegetable oil until they are tender.

3　In a greased casserole dish, layer the leek and courgette alternatively seasoning with the sea salt, freshly ground black pepper and garlic salt.

4　Preheat the oven to 350°F/180°C/gas mark 4, then make the cheese sauce.

5　Melt the butter or margarine in a pan, then remove the pan from the heat.

6　Stir in the potato flour, blending it with the butter or margarine.

7　Return the pan to the heat and add the milk and stock mixture slowly, stirring continuously until the sauce thickens.

8　Season to taste with sea salt and freshly ground black pepper, then add the nutmeg and cheese, stirring until the cheese has melted.

9　Pour the cheese sauce over the vegetables, covering them, and bake in the preheated oven for about 30 minutes.

Leek Patties

Imperial (Metric)		American
3	leeks	3
1	onion, chopped	1
1	stick celery/celery stalk, chopped	1
1	potato, peeled and sliced	1
	sea salt and freshly ground black pepper	
6-8 tbsp	matzo meal	6-8 tbsp
2	free-range eggs, beaten	2
3-4 tbsp	lemon juice	3-4 tbsp
	vegetable oil	

1 Slice off and discard the hard green parts of the leeks. Slice the remainder of the leeks, wash them very thoroughly then chop them into small pieces.

2 Steam or boil the leek, onion, celery and potato until they are tender. Drain them and squeeze out any excess liquid as the vegetable mixture must be dry. Mash the vegetables with a potato (vegetable) masher (do not use a liquidizer or food processor).

3 Season to taste with sea salt and freshly ground black pepper, then stir in the matzo meal. Mix the eggs into the mixture.

4 Chill the mixture for about 1 hour until it becomes firm. About 10 minutes before the hour is up, turn the oven on to 350°F/180°C/gas mark 4.

5 Form tablespoons of the mixture into patties and put them on greased silicone or greaseproof (waxed) paper on a large baking sheet. Sprinkle each pattie with a little lemon juice and about 1 teaspoon of oil.

6 Bake them in the preheated oven for about 30 minutes. After about 15 minutes, turn the patties over. Pour the rest of the lemon juice over the patties, and more oil if they look a little dry. Leave them to finish cooking, then serve them hot.

Note
These Leek Patties are traditionally fried, but this method is quicker, uses less oil and the patties are certainly very tasty.

Mushroom and Aubergine Casserole

Imperial (Metric)		American
1 medium	aubergine/eggplant	1 medium
	sea salt and freshly ground black pepper	
2 medium	onions, chopped	2 medium
2	cloves garlic, crushed/minced	2
	vegetable oil, for frying	
2 tbsp	tomato purée/paste	2 tbsp
½ lb (225g)	button mushrooms, chopped	3 cups
2	ripe tomatoes, skinned and chopped	2

1 Peel and slice the aubergine (eggplant). Sprinkle cut sides with salt. Layer the slices in a colander or large plate, salting each layer and leave for 30 minutes until the bitter juices have oozed out, then rinse them well and pat dry.
2 Fry the onion and garlic in a little oil until they are transparent. Stir in the tomato purée.
3 Add the aubergine (eggplant) slices and cook them until they are tender.
4 Add the mushrooms and tomatoes.
5 Season well with sea salt and freshly ground black pepper and cook gently for about 15 minutes.
6 Transfer the mixture to an ovenproof casserole dish, add a little hot water to prevent the mixture drying out, then cover the dish and keep it warm until needed or reheat it later if necessary.

Vegetable Bake

Imperial (Metric)		American
½ lb (225g)	fresh or frozen spinach	5 cups
2 medium	onions, grated/shredded or chopped	2 medium
1 small	green pepper, deseeded and chopped	1 small
1	clove garlic, crushed/minced	1
	vegetable oil, for frying	
1	stick celery/celery stalk, chopped	1
3-4 medium	carrots, grated/shredded	3-4 medium
	sea salt and freshly ground black pepper	
pinch	ground ginger	pinch
1 tbsp	tomato purée/paste	1 tbsp
2 oz (55g)	ground mixed nuts	½ cup
2	free-range eggs, beaten (optional)	2
2 oz (55g)	matzo meal	¼ cup
3 fl oz (90ml)	vegetable stock	⅓ cup

1 Wash the spinach well, cook it in a little water and then chop it finely. (Cook frozen spinach until soft.)
2 Sauté the onion, green pepper and garlic in a little oil until they have softened.
3 Preheat the oven to 350°F/180°C/gas mark 4.
4 Add the celery and carrot and cook for about 10 minutes, stirring frequently.
5 Mix all the vegetables together, season to taste with sea salt and freshly ground black pepper, add the ginger, tomato purée, nuts, eggs, if using, and the matzo meal, mixing all the ingredients together well.
6 Spoon the mixture into a greased ovenproof casserole dish and pour the hot stock over. Bake in the preheated oven for about 30 minutes until the top has browned.

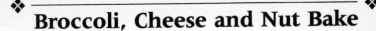

Broccoli, Cheese and Nut Bake

Imperial (Metric)		American
1 lb (455g)	broccoli, washed and divided into florets	1 lb
2	free-range eggs, beaten	2
½ lb (225g)	cottage cheese	1 cup
2 oz (55g)	grated/shredded Gouda cheese	½ cup
3 tbsp	ground almonds *or* hazelnuts	3 tbsp
2 tbsp	fine matzo meal	2 tbsp
1 tbsp	lemon juice	1 tbsp
	sea salt and freshly ground black pepper	
½ tsp	ground nutmeg	½ tsp
2 tbsp	chopped nuts	2 tbsp

1 Preheat the oven to 350°F/180°C/gas mark 4.
2 Steam or cook the broccoli in a little water until it is tender then chop it into pieces.
3 Beat the eggs and cottage cheese together.
4 Stir in the Gouda cheese, nuts, matzo meal, lemon juice and season to taste with sea salt and freshly ground black pepper and add the nutmeg.
5 Grease an ovenproof casserole dish and put the broccoli in an even layer in the bottom.
6 Spread the egg and cheese mixture over the broccoli and bake in the preheated oven for about 20 minutes. Sprinkle the nuts over the top and bake for a further 10-15 minutes.

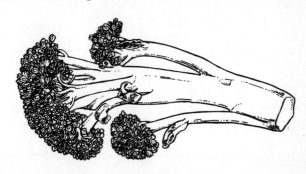

Savoury Matzo Bake

Imperial (Metric)		American
1 medium	onion, chopped	1 medium
1	clove garlic, crushed/minced	1
1 small	green pepper, deseeded and chopped	1 small
	vegetable oil, for frying	
4-5	ripe tomatoes, skinned and chopped	4-5
	sea salt and freshly ground black pepper	
	garlic salt	
2 tbsp	chopped fresh parsley	2 tbsp
5-6	matzos	5-6
2 oz (55g)	grated/shredded cheese	½ cup
10-12	mushrooms, sliced	10-12
2	free-range eggs, beaten	2
⅓ pt (200ml)	hot vegetable stock	¾ cup

1 Fry the onion, garlic and green pepper in a little of the oil until they have softened and become golden brown.
2 Add the tomatoes, season to taste with the sea salt, freshly ground black pepper and garlic salt and cook for a further 10 minutes. Add the parsley.
3 Preheat the oven to 350°F/180°C/gas mark 4.
4 Dip the matzos in water to moisten them, but not soften them.
5 Put one matzo in the bottom of a greased ovenproof casserole dish. Spoon some of the onion and tomato mixture over it. Sprinkle some of the cheese over the mixture.
6 Repeat until all the matzos, sauce and cheese have been used. Top with the mushrooms.
7 Mix the eggs well with the hot stock and pour the mixture over the layered matzos.
8 Bake in the preheated oven for about 30-40 minutes.

Gebakene Kartoffel mit Kaese
(Potato and Cheese Casserole)

Imperial (Metric)		American
2 lb (900g)	potatoes	2 lb
½ lb (225g)	cottage cheese	1 cup
2	spring onions/scallions, finely chopped	2
2 tbsp	chopped fresh parsley	2 tbsp
½ pt (285ml)	milk	1⅓ cups
	sea salt and freshly ground black pepper	
½ tsp	ground nutmeg	½ tsp
3 large	tomatoes, sliced	3 large
3 tbsp	grated/shredded Gouda cheese	3 tbsp

1 Boil the potatoes in their jackets until they are cooked. When they are cool enough to handle, peel them and cut them into small pieces.
2 Mix together the remaining ingredients, except the tomatoes and cheese.
3 Grease an ovenproof casserole dish and layer the potato, cheese mixture and tomatoes alternatively in it. Sprinkle the cheese over the top.
4 Bake in the preheated oven for about 20-30 minutes until the top is golden brown. This dish is good served with Stuffed Tomatoes (see page 178).

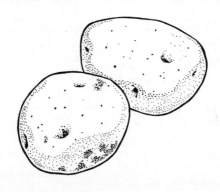

❖ Fried Mushrooms and Aubergine ❖

Imperial (Metric)		American
1 medium-large	aubergine/eggplant	1 medium-large
	sea salt and freshly ground black pepper	
4 oz (115g)	matzo meal	1 cup
1 tsp	garlic powder	1 tsp
1 tsp	paprika	1 tsp
4 oz (115g)	button mushrooms, washed	2 cups
1	free-range egg	1
	vegetable oil, for frying	

1 Peel the aubergine (eggplant), taking off as little flesh as possible as you do so, then slice the flesh, layer the slices in a colander or large plate, salting each layer, and leave for about 30 minutes until the bitter juices have oozed out. Rinse them well, then pat them dry.
2 Season the matzo meal with sea salt and freshly ground black pepper and mix in the garlic powder and paprika. Beat the egg very well.
3 Dip the aubergine (eggplant) slices and mushrooms alternately in matzo meal, beaten egg and again in matzo meal.
4 Fry them in the vegetable oil until they are golden brown.
5 Drain them on kitchen paper (paper towels).

Merren Tzimmes
(Carrot Tzimmes)

Imperial (Metric)		American
2 medium	onions, grated/shredded *or* finely chopped	2 medium
2	cloves garlic, crushed/minced	2
2 tbsp	vegetable oil	2 tbsp
1 lb (455g)	carrots, grated/shredded	1 lb
3 tbsp	ground almonds	3 tbsp
1 tsp	lemon juice	1 tsp
1	free-range egg, beaten	1
	sea salt and freshly ground black pepper	
¼ tsp	ground nutmeg	¼ tsp
2 oz (55g)	matzo meal, or as required	½ cup

1 Preheat the oven to 375°F/190°C/gas mark 5.
2 Fry the onion and garlic in the oil until they are golden brown and have become transparent.
3 Add the carrot, stirring continuously, and cook for another 5 minutes then remove the pan from the heat.
4 Combine the mixture with the almonds, lemon juice, egg, season to taste with sea salt and freshly ground black pepper and add the nutmeg.
5 Add enough matzo meal to give the mixture a firm consistency.
6 Transfer the mixture to a greased ovenproof casserole dish and bake in the preheated oven for about 30 minutes.

Tzibbale Kugel
(Onion Kugel)

Imperial (Metric)		American
4 medium	onions, finely chopped *or* grated/shredded	4 medium
2 tbsp	vegetable oil	2 tbsp
4	free-range eggs, separated	4
2 oz (55g)	matzo meal	½ cup
1 tsp	sea salt	1 tsp
¼ tsp	ground ginger	¼ tsp
	freshly ground black pepper	

1 Preheat the oven to 350°F/180°C/gas mark 4.
2 Sauté the onions in the oil until they are golden brown and have become transparent.
3 Beat the egg yolks until they are thick and creamy.
4 Mix in the sautéed onions, the oil in which they were cooked, the matzo meal, the salt and ginger and season to taste with freshly ground black pepper. Combine all the ingredients well together.
5 Beat the egg whites until they are stiff and fold them into the onion mixture with a metal spoon.
6 Gently transfer the mixture to a well-greased ovenproof dish and bake in the preheated oven for about 30-40 minutes.

Stuffed Tomatoes

Imperial (Metric)		American
4-6	firm tomatoes	4-6
4 oz (115g)	broccoli, washed	4 oz
	olive oil mixed with lemon juice, to taste	
1 tbsp	chopped fresh parsley	1 tbsp
	sea salt and freshly ground black pepper	
pinch	sugar	pinch
2 tbsp	chopped nuts	2 tbsp

1 Slice the tops off the tomatoes and scoop out the pulp, reserving it. Leave the tomatoes to drain.
2 Steam or boil the broccoli until it is tender, then cut it into small pieces. Toss it in the olive oil, lemon juice, parsley and season to taste with the sea salt, freshly ground black pepper and sugar. Stir in about 2 tablespoons of the tomato pulp (reserving the rest for use in soups and casseroles).
3 Pile the mixture into the tomato shells. Sprinkle the nuts over the stuffed tomatoes just before serving.
4 Serve them cold or hot, topped with Cheese Sauce or grated (shredded) cheese and baked for about 25-30 minutes in a preheated 350°F/180°C/gas mark 4 oven.

Geshmirte Matzo
(Cheesy Matzos)

Imperial (Metric)		American
about 12	2 by 3-in (5 by 8-cm) matzo crackers	about 12
2-3 tbsp	milk	2-3 tbsp
½ lb (225g)	cottage cheese	1 cup
2 tsp	potato flour	2 tsp
1	free-range egg, beaten	1
1 tsp	sugar	1 tsp
pinch	sea salt	pinch
½ tsp	ground cinnamon	½ tsp
extra	sugar and cinnamon to taste	extra

1 Preheat the oven to 350°F/180°C/gas mark 4.
2 Dip the matzos in the milk and remove them quickly, so that they are moistened but not softened.
3 Mix the remaining ingredients together very well, except the last, and spread the mixture over the matzos.
4 Sprinkle with extra sugar and cinnamon, according to taste, and put them on a baking sheet.
5 Bake in the preheated oven until the mixture has lightly set (about 15-20 minutes). Serve warm.

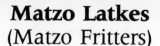

Matzo Latkes
(Matzo Fritters)

Makes about 12

Imperial (Metric)		American
4 oz (115g)	matzo meal	1 cup
1½ tbsp	ground almonds *or* hazelnuts	1½ tbsp
1 tbsp	sugar	1 tbsp
½ tsp	ground cinnamon	½ tsp
	sea salt	
2	free-range eggs, separated	2
⅓ pt (200ml)	cold water	¾ cup
	vegetable oil, for frying	

1 Mix together the matzo meal, nuts, cinnamon and sea salt to taste. Make a well in the centre of the mixture.
2 Beat the egg yolks, add the water and beat again.
3 Pour the egg and water mixture into the well in the matzo meal mixture. Stir in the well so that the dry mixture is gradually mixed in until both mixtures have been well combined. Leave the mixture to stand for 15 minutes.
4 Beat the egg whites, but not too stiffly. Fold them gently into the matzo meal mixture using a metal spoon.
5 Heat enough oil in a frying pan (skillet) and to shallow fry spoonfuls of the mixture, browning them on both sides. Serve them hot with extra ground cinnamon and a little sugar to taste.

Coconut Macaroons

Makes about 20-24

Imperial (Metric)		American
2	egg whites	2
4 oz (115g)	caster sugar	¾ cup
2 tsps	lemon juice	2 tsps
½ lb (225g)	dessicated/shredded coconut	2 cups

1. Preheat the oven to 350°F/180°C/gas mark 4.
2. Beat the egg whites until they are stiff, slowly adding the caster sugar as you do so. Add the lemon juice and beat it in.
3. Gently fold in the coconut with a metal spoon.
4. Place spoonfuls of the mixture on a greased baking sheet and shape them with damp hands as the mixture is crumbly.
5. Bake them in the preheated oven for about 15-20 minutes until they have lightly browned and are dry.

Note
The egg yolks may be added to the mixture *after* the coconut has been folded in. The macaroons will be slightly golden in colour and will take about 5-10 minutes longer to bake.

Apple Latkes

Makes about 15

Imperial (Metric)		American
3 medium	eating apples	3 medium
2 oz (55g)	matzo meal	½ cup
1 tbsp	sugar, plus extra for sprinkling	1 tbsp
1	free-range egg, beaten	1
pinch	ground cinnamon, plus extra for sprinkling	pinch
	sea salt	
	vegetable oil, for frying	

1. Peel the apples and grate (shred) them.
2. Combine the apple with the rest of the ingredients except the oil, mixing everything together well.
3. Chill the mixture for about 20 minutes.
4. Place spoonfuls of the mixture into hot oil in frying pan (skillet) and brown them on both sides.
5. Drain them on kitchen paper (paper towels).
6. Serve them hot with cinnamon and sugar sprinkled over them.

Banana and Hazelnut Fritters

Makes about 12-15

Imperial (Metric)		American
4	ripe bananas	4
1	free-range egg, beaten	1
4 oz (115g)	matzo meal	1 cup
3 tbsp	ground hazelnuts	3 tbsp
1 tbsp	sugar	1 tbsp
1 tsp	ground cinnamon	1 tsp
	vegetable oil, for frying	

1 Mash the bananas well, then mix in the egg.
2 Mix the matzo meal, ground hazelnuts, sugar and cinnamon into the banana and egg mixture.
3 Chill the mixture for 30 minutes.
4 Heat a little oil in a frying pan (skillet).
5 Drop tablespoonfuls of the banana mixture into the pan and fry them on both sides.
6 Serve the fritters hot, with cinnamon and sugar sprinkled over them or with natural (unsweetened) yogurt.

Pesach Apple and Nut Pudding

Imperial (Metric)		American
4	free-range eggs	4
	sea salt	
4 oz (115g)	sugar	⅔ cup
3-4	eating apples, grated/shredded	3-4
1 oz (30g)	matzo meal	¼ cup
1 oz (30g)	ground almonds	¼ cup
3-4 tbsp	chopped almonds	3-4 tbsp

1 Preheat the oven to 350°F/180°C/gas mark 4.
2 Separate the eggs. Beat the whites with a pinch of sea salt until they are stiff then set them aside.

3   Beat the yolks and sugar together until they are light and creamy. Add the apple, matzo meal and ground almonds. Fold the egg whites into the mixture gently with a metal spoon.
4   Pour the mixture into a greased pie dish. Sprinkle the almonds over the top and bake in the preheated oven for about 40 minutes.

Plavah
(Passover Cake)

Makes one 9-in (23-cm) cake

Imperial (Metric)		American
4	free-range eggs	4
6 oz (170g)	caster/superfine or granulated sugar	1 cup
2 tsp	lemon juice	2 tsp
3 oz (85g)	fine matzo meal	¾ cup
pinch	sea salt	pinch
	caster sugar, for dusting	

1   Preheat the oven to 350°F/180°C/gas mark 4 and prepare a 9-in (23-cm) round tin (pan) by greasing it well and lining it with greaseproof (waxed) paper and greasing it again.
2   Separate the eggs. Beat the yolks and sugar together until they are pale and creamy.
3   Add the lemon juice, matzo meal and the sea salt.
4   Beat the whites until they are stiff and fold them gently into the egg mixture with a metal spoon.
5   Bake in the prepared tin in the preheated oven for about 40-45 minutes until it is golden brown and cooked through. Test whether the cake is done by inserting a knife or skewer in the middle; if it comes out dry, the cake is done.
6   Dust the top of the cake with caster sugar.

Variation:
Bake the cake mixture in two sandwich tins (layer cake pans) for about 25-30 minutes. Sandwich the cakes together with whipped cream or fromage frais and crushed strawberries.

Pesach Chocolate Nut Squares

Imperial (Metric)		American
2	free-range eggs	2
5 oz (140g)	sugar	¾ cup
1 tbsp	Sabra liqueur (optional)	1 tbsp
2 oz (55g)	dark/bitter chocolate	2 oz
4 oz (115g)	butter *or* polyunsaturated margarine	½ cup
2 oz (55g)	fine matzo meal	½ cup
3 oz (85g)	chopped nuts	⅔ cup
pinch	sea salt	pinch

1 Preheat the oven to 325°F/170°C/gas mark 3.
2 Beat the eggs and sugar together until the mixture is light and creamy. Add the liqueur at this point, if using, and beat again.
3 Melt the chocolate in a saucepan resting in a larger pan with some slowly boiling water in it.
4 Add the butter or margarine, melt it and mix it in well. Let it cool, resting the saucepan in a bowlful of cold water for 5 minutes.
5 Combine the cooled chocolate mixture with the egg mixture.
6 Add the matzo meal a little at a time, stirring it in well each time, then add the nuts and salt.
7 Pour the mixture in to a well greased 7 by 11-in (18 by 28-cm) tin (pan) and bake in the preheated oven for about 20-30 minutes. Cut it into squares while it is still warm.

Apple and Pear Crumble

Imperial (Metric)		American
5	apples, peeled and sliced	5
3	pears, peeled and sliced	3
6 tbsp	orange juice	6 tbsp
¼ tsp	ground cinnamon	¼ tsp
1-2 tbsp	strawberry jam/jelly	1-2 tbsp
	Crumble topping	
4 tbsp	medium matzo meal	4 tbsp
4 tbsp	ground almonds	4 tbsp
3 tbsp	dessicated/shredded coconut	3 tbsp
2 tbsp	sugar	2 tbsp
2 oz (55g)	polyunsaturated margarine, plus extra as required	¼ cup

1 Poach the apple and pear slices in the orange juice, until they are tender. Sprinkle the cinnamon over them.
2 Spoon the fruit and the cooking juices into a greased ovenproof dish. Mix in the strawberry jam.
3 Preheat the oven to 375°F/190°C/gas mark 5.
4 Now make the crumble topping. Mix the dry ingredients together and cut in the margarine, blending it until the mixture resembles fine breadcrumbs.
5 Spread it over the fruit in the dish and dot the top with margarine.
6 Bake in the preheated oven for about 30 minutes or until the topping has cooked and is golden brown.

Passover Almond Meringue Tart

Makes one 6 by 9-in (15 by 23-cm) tart

Imperial (Metric)		American
	Pastry	
3 oz (85g)	fine matzo meal	¾ cup
3 oz (85g)	potato flour	¾ cup
1 oz (30g)	ground nuts	¼ cup
1	free-range egg, lightly beaten	1
2 oz (55g)	soft, polyunsaturated margarine	¼ cup
2-3 tbsp	cold water	2-3 tbsp
4 tbsp	sugar	4 tbsp
1 tsp	lemon juice	1 tsp
	Filling	
2 oz (55g)	polyunsaturated margarine	¼ cup
8 tbsp	sugar	8 tbsp
2	free-range egg yolks	2
4 oz (115g)	ground almonds	1 cup
2	free-range egg whites	2

1 Preheat the oven to 400°F/200°C/gas mark 6.
2 First make the pastry. Mix the dry ingredients together in a bowl. Make a well and blend in the egg, margarine and water. Knead the dough until it forms a smooth ball. Put it in the bowl, cover and chill it for 10 minutes. Use half the dough (freezing the rest) for a thin crust or all of it for a thicker crust.
3 Roll it out and line a 6 by 9-in (15 by 23-cm) greased pie dish, raising the sides slightly, and prick it with a fork. Bake it blind (see page 17) in the preheated oven for 15-20 minutes until it is golden brown. Turn the oven down to 350°F/180°C/gas mark 4.
4 Now make the filling. Beat the margarine and the 5 tablespoons of the sugar together until they are creamy.
5 Add the egg yolks and beat the mixture well again.
6 Add the ground almonds and beat them into the mixture.
7 Spread the mixture over the bottom of the pastry case (shell).

8 Beat the egg whites until they are stiff and gently fold in the rest of the sugar.
9 Spread this mixture lightly and evenly over the filling.
10 Bake in the preheated oven for about 20 minutes then turn the oven down to 300°F/150°C/gas mark 2 and bake for 5-10 more minutes.

Ingberlach
(Sweets/Candies)

Imperial (Metric)		American
1½ lb (680g)	carrots	1½ lb
1 lb (455g)	sugar	1 lb
4 tbsp	orange juice	4 tbsp
1 tsp	ground cinnamon	1 tsp
1 tsp	ground ginger	1 tsp
4 oz (115g)	ground *or* chopped nuts	1 cup

1 Finely grate (shred) the carrots.
2 Over a medium heat, cook the carrots, sugar, orange juice, cinnamon and ginger, stirring often so that it does not stick. After about 30 minutes, add the nuts.
3 Cook for about 20 more minutes over a low heat, continuing to stir it often. Remove the pan from the heat. The mixture should be fairly thick.
4 Line a 6 by 9-in (15 by 23-cm) tin (pan) with greaseproof (waxed) paper and spread the mixture over it to a thickness of about ½ inch (1cm). When it has cooled completely, cut it into squares, sprinkle sugar or dessicated (shredded) coconut over the top and serve as sweets.

Carrot and Nut Cake

Makes one 9-10-in (23-25.5-cm) cake

Imperial (Metric)		American
½ lb (225g)	sugar	1 cup
2 oz (55g)	potato flour	½ cup
2 oz (55g)	fine matzo meal	½ cup
2 oz (55g)	ground almonds	½ cup
4 oz (115g)	dessicated/shredded coconut	1 cup
1 tsp	Passover baking powder	1 tsp
1 tsp	ground cinnamon	1 tsp
¾ lb (340g)	carrots, grated/shredded finely	2 cups
4 fl oz (115ml)	vegetable oil	½ cup
4 fl oz (115ml)	hot water	½ cup
3	free-range eggs	3
4 oz (115g)	chopped walnuts/English walnuts	½ cup

1   Preheat the oven to 350°F/180°C/gas mark 4.
2   Mix together all the dry ingredients, except the walnuts, and
    stir in the carrot. Make a well in middle and pour in oil, hot
    water and eggs.
3   Mix everything together well and beat the mixture gently for
    about 5 minutes.
4   Stir in the walnuts.
5   Pour the mixture into a greased 9-10-in (23-25.5-cm) round
    cake tin (pan) and smooth the top.
6   Bake in the preheated oven for about 60 minutes or until it
    is cooked through. It is done when a knife or skewer inserted
    into the middle of the cake comes out clean.

*Try some of these Passover recipes at other times of the year – they are
delicious.*

Suggestions for menus for Sabbath and Festival meals

Lunch, winter

Challah (p.150)
Danish 'Hirring' in Sweet and Sour Sauce (p.22)
Hobernergroten Soup (Oat and Vegetable Soup) (p.39)
Cholent and Knaidel (p.95)
Potato Kugel (p.108)
Galuptzi (Spicy Cabbage Rolls) (p.86)
Cabbage and Apple Salad (p.120)
Carrot and Pineapple Salad (p.125)
Pears in Wine (p.133)
Walnut Tart (p.144)

Lunch, summer

Challah (p.150)
Mock Petzah (Savoury Jelly) (p.30)
Galia Soup (p.48)
Aubergine Quiche (p.87) or
Mock Seafood Mayonnaise (p.81)
Mock Salmon Rissoles (p.57)
Potato Salad (p.122)
Garden Salad (p.114)
Avocado and Papaya Salad (p.117)
Mango Fool (p.129)
Sugariyot Sumsum (Sesame Bites) (p.141)

Evening meal, winter

Challah (p.150)
Mock Chopped Liver II (p.26)
Clear Vegetable Soup (p.35)
Kneidlach (Soup dumplings) (p.52)
Savoury Lentil and Vegetable Strudel (p.83)
Carrot and Potato Tzimmes (p.112)
Fasoulia (Sephardic Green Beans) (p.111)
Roast potatoes or Potato Kugel (p.108)
Cholemady (Pickled Vegetables) (p.115)
Fruit Whip (p.139)
Hungarian Cherry Cake (p.145)

Evening meal, summer

Challah (p.150)
Mock Chopped Herring (p.21)
Onion and Tomato Soup (p.40)
Cashew Nut Casserole (Mock Chicken Casserole) (p.56)
Plain brown rice or Orez Parsi (p.104)
Courgettes and Tomatoes (p.106) or
Spinach Soufflé (p.101)
Celery Salad (p.121)
Cherry and Lychee Delight (p.137)
Apple Farfel Tart (p.143)

Index